Good Grad!

*A Practical Guide to Graduate School
in the Sciences & Engineering*

Joseph W. Gangestad, Ph.D.

TESSERAL
PRESS

ISBN-13: 978-0-9889726-0-5 (pbk.)

Contents

Acknowledgments

My most heartfelt thanks belong first and foremost to my wife, Danielle, who has suffered through many arduous conversations about this book with her usual grace and aplomb. Her patience with my rambling, blathering, and agonizing over the composition of this book cannot be matched.

I also owe a great debt to my graduate advisor, Professor James Longuski, who always took the time to help mold his students into professionals, from refining journal articles to constructing a resume. Prof. Longuski maintained a policy of openness and personal support that I will always respect and attempt to emulate.

Although this book is about graduate school, I cannot neglect to acknowledge my undergraduate advisor, Prof. Jay Pasachoff, who set me on my way professionally and has been an invaluable mentor, both during college and since. His guidance in my early years put me on the path to success in grad school, and I am thankful for his ongoing support of my career.

Lastly, many thanks to my friends and colleagues from grad school who were kind enough to read this book through several drafts. It takes the perspectives of more than one person to make a useful guide, and this book couldn't have happened without you.

Introduction

I wish I had asked more questions when I was planning for grad school. I preoccupied myself by studying research programs and faculty. I worried about picking a university with a reputable name. I studied course catalogs and credit requirements. No one warned me about the other questions I should have asked: about day-to-day life as a grad student, about research lab politics, about attending conferences and publishing journal articles, about finding an advisor and securing funding. I had no idea about the sexual and racial tensions that swirl around research labs. I never realized politics can have as much impact on publications as experiments do. And who knew that picking the right advisor and committee can make the difference of a year or more on your graduation time?

Undergraduate programs offer almost no guidance on what graduate school is like. Professors rarely advise anyone on the inner workings of grad school, but they are happy to encourage you to sign up anyway. Every year, 500,000 students in the United States graduate with a bachelor's degree in the sciences and engineering, and more than 100,000 of them enroll in graduate school. For most, grad school is a trial by fire: full of rituals, formalities, and milestones for which you receive little or no warning and precious few resources to guide you through.

I used to volunteer as a mentor for these new and prospective grad students. Every year, a new crop of students asked me the same questions about the university, about my advisor, about classes. Every year, I gave them the same answers. With the end of my years in grad school approaching, I decided to consolidate those answers in one place, plus answer all the questions no one thought to ask.

I was frustrated to find that most resources about grad school focus on the beginning, when you're working on an application, or on the end, when you're looking for a job. But there are years—maybe more than a half-decade—between those two bookends, when you're just surviving daily life as a grad student. For most of your time in grad school, you're not worrying about looking good to an admissions committee or beefing up a resume. You're hoping that you'll get that teaching position next semester so you can pay the rent; you're working late into the night to get that conference abstract submitted before the deadline; you're wondering how to get forms signed when your advisor is out of town; you're hoping you won't have to spend the weekend in lab. To do your "job" as a grad student, you have to go to conferences, write journal articles, navigate collaborations, indulge eccentric professors, teach undergraduates, and secure funding for yourself every semester. Undergrad teaches you none of these skills, and no one warns you before you start grad school that you need them.

Science and engineering often find themselves at odds, but the experience in grad school for both disciplines is very similar. In contrast, the experience in the humanities is so fundamentally different that there is no way one book can honestly and effectively cover them both. In this book you will find discussions on life in a research lab, on attending science and engineering conferences, on the dance between author and reviewer of a journal article, and on preparing your master's or Ph.D. defense. A humanities student in an M.A. program would approach these tasks very differently from how they are described here.

This book contains practical and politically incorrect wisdom that my fellow grad students and I picked up over four or five (or six) years working on our master's degrees and Ph.D.'s. I have tried to select advice and observations that are more or less universal for grad students in the sciences and engineering. I cannot tell you how to do discipline-specific research, but I can warn you about petty rivalries, inconsiderate colleagues who borrow your equipment without permission, collaborations that are lop-sided in responsibility but not credit, and Friday nights spent feeding the lab rats. I also don't name names: there are no recommendations on specific graduate schools academically, geographically, or demographically, but I can discuss how the size or location of a university may affect your life as a grad student. A fit for grad school is a personal one, and no ranked list in a magazine can make that judgment for you.

After you've read this book, I hope it doesn't discourage you from attending grad school. No matter what you choose to do at this stage of your life—grad school, work, the Peace Corps, itinerant minstrel—every path has its warts and downsides; those for grad school (and the ways to cope with them) happen to be documented here. Challenges and frustrations aside, the grad-school experience teaches you how to work and think independently and how to become a fully functioning member of a profession. Grad school is not for everyone, but if it is for you, it is a rewarding experience, and you will walk away with accomplishments, titles, and self-confidence that no amount of money can buy. However, there is no patented "path to success," and if you're looking for one, you shouldn't be considering grad school in the first place. Grad school is about going through these experiences and figuring them out for yourself. This book is simply a heads-up.

Chapter 1

Going to Grad School

At first blush, grad school appears very similar to life as an undergraduate. You are still "in school." You are still a student. For your first year or two, you might even say that you're still "in college," especially if it's too much trouble to explain the difference to your relatives. Classes, homework, and exams come and go with the semesters. Most of your professors remain aloof and favor their research over planning eloquent lectures. If you don't change schools, your social circle may very well remain intact, too.

Undergrad was a time to learn independence, experiment with a potpourri of man-made substances and lifestyles, develop a robust and tightly knit social life, and be introduced to academic disciplines that may or may not have any bearing on your future. Universities have structured their academics and woven their social fabric to facilitate post-pubescent enlightenment. Undergrad offers a gentle initiation into adulthood. But when you finally graduate with a bachelor's degree, you cannot be part of that club again. If you try to hold on to that spirited time as an undergrad, you eventually transform into the crusty alum who can't grow up.

Grad school is both the start of your real life and a postponement of it, a sort of purgatory before adulthood. Unless you already have a regular job and return to university for work-related education, grad school ensures that you can hold off the job search for another two or four or six years. After more than twenty years of growing up and living in an academic setting (from grade school to middle school to high school to college), grad school is comforting in its familiarity. You know how merit and advancement are measured in academia. You are familiar with the pulse of daily academic life. If you've made it through college and are considering grad school immediately thereafter, you are probably very good at doing the "right" things to succeed in school.

But despite its perpetuation of the student life, grad school is also where your career starts. A bachelor's degree in chemistry qualifies you for many jobs that only require critical thinking, but signing up for a chemistry Ph.D. is a commitment to becoming a *professional*. Once you've achieved that advanced degree, the field becomes your career, and you become an active member of a community devoted to your discipline. No one can force you to stay, but after so much investment of time and effort, you will be loath to give it up. You don't find many physics Ph.D.'s writing operas.

While you are in grad school, the emphasis is on your personal responsibility to seek the classes, mentorship, and guidance you need to enter the army of professionals in your field. Your professors will become your peers and colleagues. You ultimately have to demonstrate, through research, presentations, and publications, that you have made a contribution to the field and deserve to be part of the club. Undergrad has graded homework and exams with right or wrong answers, but grad school has no answer key, and the path to success (or graduation) is seldom clear.

Why Go to Grad School?

When weighing whether to attend grad school, one frequently encounters advice to weigh pros and cons, to calculate tuition budgets, or to chart personal goals. For most undergrads, the choice actually happens organically over the last year or two of college, in which it becomes increasingly clear to you whether grad school is a good or bad idea. Aside from those returning to school from the working world, applying to grad school leans more in the direction of "gut feeling" than it does any reasoned decision. There are plenty of resources out there to help you decide whether you should go to grad school and which ones to apply to, and those resources provide excellent source material for an application essay, which must be sober and mature. However, they usually give only a wink and a nod to the "real" reasons most people get an advanced degree: money, inertia, and vanity.

An advanced degree in the sciences and engineering really can increase your earning potential. An undergraduate degree provides you with a strong foundation in a subject area, but seldom does it bestow on you anything useful to an employer. An advanced degree provides practical skills (for example, how to operate equipment in a functioning research lab, rather than in the carefully structured "theater" of college science classes) and signals to an employer that you have at least some experience working independently to achieve a goal (i.e., your degree). The higher your degree, the more valuable you become by virtue of your greater depth of knowledge, your experience, and your problem-solving skills. In many engineering disciplines, each additional degree nets you about 30% higher salary.

Furthermore, an advanced degree raises the height of institutional glass ceilings. Many jobs in science and engineering only entertain candidates with advanced degrees, and this condition is becoming more common every year. With only a bachelor's degree, you will probably reach a career position where you can rise no higher because of bureaucratic rules about degree requirements (whether they make sense or not). In some institutional cultures you need a Ph.D. if you want to manage other Ph.D.'s. For every college dropout who makes millions tinkering in his parents' garage, there are dozens of work-a-day scientists and engineers who must actually live within the bureaucratic culture and get that advanced degree.

Although career advancement is a reasonable motivation for grad school, "inertia" must certainly be the most common. Every book on the subject of grad school wants you to make a reasoned decision in which you map out the course of your life and seek out happiness and self-actualization by pursuing the noble goal of studying a field that you love. Most of us go to grad school—and in particular those who go straight out of undergrad—because "it's what everyone else is doing." For better or worse, a culture has formed in undergraduate institutions where it is simply expected that the most successful and technically minded individuals go to grad school. It's what the "smart people" do. If you've done well in the sciences or engineering and enjoy it, grad school is what you're supposed to do, the culture says. You would be hard pressed to find a professor or career counselor who recommends taking your *summa cum laude* B.S. in biology and applying for jobs in the pharmaceutical industry.

Inertia is not a terrible reason for grad school. Most of undergrad is a whirlwind of subjects touched on lightly, enough to get your feet wet. Many or even most people don't know what they want to do after college. It is unfair, even after years of college, to expect someone to know exactly what he or she wants to do in life and to seek out the appropriate institution with a dispassionate calculus. My own professors in college, seasoned by years of research, confessed that they still sometimes questioned what field they wanted to work in. Many decisions in life are made on feelings and the force of inertia. If you've made it this far, it's a good sign that you can roll with the punches and make the best of where the currents of life send you. If you enjoyed certain subjects in undergrad, then grad school is an adequate place to see if they're appropriate for you professionally. There's a good chance you'll find something that you enjoy, and the advanced degree will make you that much more attractive to employers when you finish. If grad school doesn't agree with you, you can always leave and seek out a real job.

A third and final politically incorrect reason for grad school: vanity. More than a few grad students are guilty of lusting after the title of "doctor." When you earn that title after years of hard work, no one can take it away from you. You can put it on your credit card, your license, and your return-address labels. If most of your friends are also on their way to a Ph.D., social pressure builds to join the club yourself. Is vanity a good reason to *start* a grad program? Probably not. There are many cheaper ways to get extra letters before or after your name. However, after you've been in grad school for a few years—after all the blood, sweat, toil, and tears, and after all of your original excuses for going to grad school have been lost to the depths of time—vanity may be the one thing that keeps you going.

The choice between going to work and going to grad school is a challenging one. If you can't get a job after undergrad (say, because of a bad economy), grad school is a popular refuge to wait out the storm. Usually, you can get some funding in the sciences and engineering, even if only as a teaching assistant, which is more work than you might get in the real world. Nonetheless, you will invariably compare yourself, the lowly grad student, to your friends who went to get jobs. The amount of money they make will astonish you in comparison to what the university pays.

If you are already working and wish to start (or restart) grad school, the transition could be jarring. Many employers have work-study and workplace-advancement programs that pay for some or all of an advanced degree. This free money frequently incurs additional years of required employment at the company, but it is far preferable to taking a major pay cut and becoming a full-time graduate student. Distance-learning classes have become so popular at many universities—because they are cheap to produce and because companies pay full-price tuition—that most students can get a degree without ever stepping foot on campus. The downside to getting another degree while working is the time it will take. A full-time grad student can get a master's degree in two years or so. A full-time employee has time for perhaps only one class per semester, and a master's degree could take twice as long. Employees working on a Ph.D. might need an extra two or three years to finish the academic requirements and dissertation while satisfying their employer's full-time demands.

I recommend only one calculation when choosing between grad school and work: the opportunity cost. That is, the amount of money in potential wages you give up to attend grad school. Consider the yearly salary you might have made if you went straight to work with your bachelor's degree. You can use your friends and colleagues as reasonable benchmarks. Multiply that salary by 2 years for a master's degree or by 5 (and possibly more) for a Ph.D., and subtract the amount you expect to be paid over those years as a research or teaching assistant. That is—approximately—the opportunity cost of grad school. Here's a numerical example: estimate your friends in the real world are making $50,000 a year, but you only get paid $17,000 as a teaching assistant. After your two years of a master's degree, your friends have made $100,000 (taxes notwithstanding) but you only earned $34,000; the difference is the opportunity cost, $66,000. That's the cost in lost earnings of attending grad school.

Table 1 summarizes an example opportunity cost calculation for a master's degree and Ph.D. The salaries and graduation times that apply to you depend on your field and may deviate significantly from this table: a grad student on a fellowship (instead of

Table 1: The Opportunity Cost of Grad School

Master's degree

Earned by working	$50K/yr × 2 yrs =	$100K
Earned as grad student	$17K/yr × 2 yrs =	−($34K)
Opportunity cost:		$66K

Ph.D.

Earned by working	$50K/yr × 5 yrs =	$250K
Earned as grad student	$17K/yr × 5 yrs =	−($85K)
Opportunity cost:		$165K

working as a teaching assistant) may receive as much as $30K per year on a stipend, a Ph.D. could last a lot longer than 5 years, or a bachelor's degree in your field may earn more or less than $50K per year. Either way, the opportunity cost of grad school is easily in the tens and hundreds of thousands of dollars. But be sure not to confuse the opportunity cost, which is the money you *forgo* to attend grad school, with the actual cost, which is the amount you pay for grad school in tuition, fees, and other materials. The opportunity cost is probably much higher than the actual cost, especially when you account for tuition wavers as a teaching or research assistant (more on the costs of grad school in Chapter 6).

However, there is a silver lining to this dark cloud. Next estimate the extra earnings over your lifetime with the advanced degree, compared to a salary with just a bachelor's degree. Odds are that the number will be much higher. Back to the example: with your shiny new master's degree, you're making $75,000 a year now, while your friends are still stuck at $50,000 (ignoring inflation and raises). That's a $25,000-a-year advantage you have, making up for the opportunity cost of grad school in less than 3 years. In the sciences and engineering, you can typically make up the opportunity cost of grad school in only 5 years of work. That leaves 30 or more years of substantially improved earnings.

Master's vs. Ph.D.

Your decision to attend graduate school at all may not be nearly as hard as the choice you make later between pursuing a master's degree or a Ph.D. Many grad students begin a master's program without hesitation but spend a year or more paralyzed by the decision to continue to a Ph.D. The lure of the Ph.D. is strong, but the commitment is great. Some grad students start a Ph.D. program and realize soon thereafter that their heart isn't in it enough to justify the additional years of work. Although an external force like the economy may make the original choice for you between work and grad school, the choice to *continue* in grad school is one of those big life decisions. Some people know their goal from the beginning; for others, it takes more exposure to the life of the grad student to swing the pendulum one way or the other.

The master's degree, which is one step "above" your bachelor's degree, is usually completed in about two years, depending on your advisor (if you have one at all), the field of study, and other factors. The master's is the typical "working" degree for engineering. That is, most engineers in the workplace have a master's degree. You will find master's degrees all the way to the top of engineering management in most companies, even the largest. On the other hand, a master's degree has little cachet in the sciences. Aside from those planning on going into teaching (in high school, not at the university level), there are few jobs out there where a master's in chemistry or physics is preferred. Rather, the master's degree is a common consolation prize in the sciences for individuals who don't finish their Ph.D. After a few years of toil in a Ph.D. program, if it becomes clear that you won't finish (for any number of personal or academic reasons), many departments will offer you a master's degree. That way you have something to show for your time and at least have an edge applying for a teaching position.

A master's degree program may offer a choice between thesis and non-thesis options. A thesis is by far the most common, but non-thesis is sometimes available in engineering programs. A non-thesis master's program is little different from a miniature undergraduate experience. You take three or four semesters of classes, two or three classes per semester, and graduate automatically when the academic requirements are completed. A master's thesis, on the other hand, is like a miniature Ph.D. experience, in which you define a project, perform the research, experiments, and analysis, write up your results, and defend them before a faculty committee. A master's thesis project is on a smaller scale than a Ph.D. and takes less time. Many theses reproduce or minimally extend the research of someone else, rather than make a major contribution to the field.

The Ph.D. is the highest degree anyone can achieve, and once you have it, as a matter of credentials you are a peer with all of the other professors and experts out there. The Ph.D. takes at least four years beyond the bachelor's degree, more typically five or six, and not uncommonly more than that. Ph.D. research is open-ended. Your advisor doesn't know the "answer" to your research problem any more than you do, and there may be no clear-cut answer at all. Experiments may go wrong. New tangents may prove more fruitful than the originally defined project. A Ph.D. is done when it's done. Knowing whether it's done is a subtle skill that develops over years as a grad student. Later chapters will discuss how the progress of your research, your relationship with your advisor, and input from your committee eventually lead to a consensus on the completion of your degree.

The Ph.D. is distinguished from the master's degree by performing original, peer-reviewed research in your field. Publication of your research (or, at least, the publishability of your research) is the arbiter for the completion of the Ph.D. The line between a master's degree and a Ph.D. is sometimes blurry. Many master's theses have publishable material, but not in enough quantity nor of enough import to impress a faculty committee. Although it sounds like you are at the mercy of capricious faculty over whether you're doing Ph.D.-worthy research, once you are in the program for a while you get a feel for what makes a Ph.D. (This question will come up in later chapters.) Perhaps the best phrase to describe a Ph.D.'s worth of work is, to borrow a quote from Justice Potter Stewart, "I know it when I see it."*

A Ph.D. is an enormous commitment. You really need to enjoy, if not love, the subject material. You were exposed to it in

---

*Justice Stewart famously coined this phrase in a censorship case before the United States Supreme Court, in which he used it to describe the threshold test for pornography. Its use in the context of this book seems equally appropriate.

undergraduate, but your first year of grad school will crystallize your feelings towards the field. If, after a year of grad school, you're still on the fence about the subject, Ph.D. program or otherwise, it's unlikely that you'll come around to it in another year or three. If you're lucky enough to find a subject that you love, the Ph.D. program lets you enjoy it to excess. In exchange for basking in your field of choice for four or five years, you live in quasi-indentured servitude, working as a teaching or research assistant for your advisor, who gets his name on everything you do.

A Ph.D. is not an unqualified ticket to future success. Many disciplines outside academia regard a Ph.D. as an *over* qualification, especially in engineering. The Ph.D. can be perceived as an academic credential, with its holder having spent too much time in the theoretical world of a research lab instead of gaining real-world experience that a company can use. An employee with a Ph.D. is more expensive, but the work he or she does is often the same as that of a master's-degree hire. Many companies don't see the benefit in dollars and cents. As you consider entering a Ph.D. program, you should be mindful of your career goals, or at least contemplate what career options are available given your field. If industry hates hiring Ph.D.'s but you insist on getting one anyway, you may have to accept being stuck on the academic track.

Those students fortunate enough to know from the very beginning that they want a Ph.D. may have the option of entering a Ph.D. program directly from undergrad. Direct-to-Ph.D. programs are typical in the sciences, where master's degrees are uncommon. However, not all departments or universities may give you that option. You may have to get your master's degree first, as an entirely separate affair, before you are allowed to enter the Ph.D. program.

These different systems in part revolve around the question of funding. With direct-to-Ph.D., a cash-strapped department—which is most of them these days—can identify the most committed students in a separate Ph.D. program to give preference with teaching and research positions. Many clever grad students enter a Ph.D. program as soon as they can, regardless of their actual degree plans, to increase the probability of getting funded by the department. For the same reason, a direct-to-Ph.D. program may be very difficult to leave. After making a direct-to-Ph.D. commitment to the department, which rewards you with a minuscule salary, it may be impossible to escape early with anything to show for it. You might get the "door prize" master's degree, but the department has a vested interest in making that a painful process.

Where Should You Go?

If you decide graduate school is right for you, you have to select a handful of schools to apply to, but that task is markedly different from when you sought a college for undergrad. You have to identify a discipline that interests you, and you may have to be very specific. If you majored as an undergraduate in biology, graduate programs may require you to choose between biochemistry, genetics, ecology, microbiology, zoology, and more, which may be all in separate departments with separate degrees. Undergrad was a time for academic experimentation, but grad school is for specialization. Changing departments is rare once you are in a program, and a careful review of any particular department's offerings is paramount before you apply.

Grad school is, in general, not about big names. Having a bachelor's degree from an Ivy League school or a big state university is a source of pride, but those names don't carry the same weight on a graduate degree. Your productivity in research—and the professional reputation you develop—is driven more by your advisor and your specific department than by the university. One school that does not rank highly in famous top-ten lists may nonetheless have a world-renowned electrical engineering program, whereas electrical engineering at an old and ivy-bestrewn university in New England may not even be on the map. If you're looking to become a great electrical engineer, the famous name won't do much for you. Most people, if they judge you at all, will be more interested in who your advisor is than the school you go to.

Even more important than the reputation of a particular department is the research that its faculty is doing. If a highly respected department of chemists has no one researching your area of interest, then the school has nothing to offer you. On the other hand, if you find a faculty member doing niche research that you have a passion for, but it's at a small, less renowned university, you should give it the most serious consideration. The prestige of a famous name cannot make up for research that you hate. If you pick your grad program for the name alone (like picking a job only for the money), you may end up miserable. Do research you enjoy, no matter where you must do it, and you will produce far better results than if you go somewhere you hate.

Choosing the right grad school for you involves trade-offs, one of which is between big universities and smaller institutions. The large research university is a machine, whose main purpose is to attract buckets of research money, generate volumes of press-release worthy research, and churn out graduates whom they can tap for alumni donations. Large schools have lots of professors and, usually, lots of funding to go around. You are surrounded by over-caffeinated grad students (most of whom come from a different country with a more zealous work ethic than yours), all competing against you to get into the well-funded research groups with the famous professors.

The focus at these institutions is research and funding, which feed the leviathan of university bureaucracy (see Chapter 9) and its bloated roster of deans and administrators. This arrangement is beneficial to grad students who find themselves a funded lab, but not so good for students in a classroom. Professors are hired and tenured based on the quality and quantity of research funding, rather than on their teaching ability. Classes are often large, anonymous affairs, and even graduate-level classes may be taught by senior graduate students. An individual professor or two may stand out for their top-notch teaching, but they are not the norm.

Smaller universities hold more promise for providing personal attention. They also typically set a higher standard for the teaching skills of the faculty, which makes your own classes more rewarding. These schools market the quality of their education, rather than the number of named professor chairs, and hire and retain faculty with an eye to maintaining that standard. At a small school with less competition among grad students, you can more easily distinguish yourself and take on responsibility quickly. In a small research group, you could quickly rise up the ranks and be in charge in a few years, working closely with your advisor on classes, research, and grant proposals.

Unfortunately, small universities have less academic diversity, simply because of their size. If you find that you don't enjoy a particular path of research, there may not be many other groups to choose from, and if there are, there may not be enough funding to accommodate you.

Private versus public academic institutions is another trade-off. A private school almost invariably has access to more resources, buoyed by a century or more of compound interest on its eternally growing, alumni-supported endowment. Private funding and plum endowments offer more perks and a freer flow of cash. A posh, private university in the Northeast is more likely to have free events and food, swanky and wood-paneled reading rooms, plentiful funding for student groups, and top-of-the-line facilities than its state-sponsored counterparts. Private universities tend to carry more prestige (if we're talking strictly about names), but there is also volatility due to fluctuations in the endowment. A bad year on Wall Street could leave your private university in the red, putting classes and your funding (and the free food) at risk.

A public university, on the other hand, is a slave to the budgets of state government, and the bureaucracy can be oppressive. In bad years, the government reduces funding to balance its budget, and administrators are dispatched to cry foul and claim penny-pinching politicians are crippling education in the state. Somehow, after decades of such prognostications year in and year out, doomsday never comes, and the politicians, who use the public universities as a jobs program for political allies, always find a way to keep them running. On the positive side, public universities are usually half the price of a private school, or even less, especially for in-state students.

Before you apply to any grad school, you have a lot of homework to do. You have a feeling for whether you want to attend a large or a small school, or what discipline you want to study, but every department and research group is different. Applying to grad school is very similar to applying for a job. Before you go in, you need to know exactly what you're getting yourself into. You need to identify where you would fit into the machine, what your responsibilities would be, who you would work for and with, and how long you think you would be there. That means getting details down to the individual professors and other grad students, which will give you a complete picture of the world you would inhabit for several years. Later chapters address these issues in greater detail.

The most straightforward way to get the information you need is, as always, from the Internet. Universities' and departments' front-page websites have institutional information, like deadlines, degree requirements, lists of labs, and self-serving statistics, but it's the professors' websites where the useful information can be found. Unlike institutional websites, which almost always conform to the university's corporate standard (and yes, they are corporate in spirit if not in fact), most group- or advisor-level websites are individually managed and have more personality. By reading through these websites you get a feel for what each professor does, who they work with, and whether you think you could fit in that environment.

Each professor's list of recent publications is a looking glass into that research group. Not every professor regularly updates the content of their website, but nearly every professor makes sure to list their most recent publications. A professor's "research interests" section is likely littered with topics that the professor no longer actively researches. If he or she still has expertise in a particular area with a history of publications, that subject may retain a bullet point on the list even though the professor hasn't touched that work in a decade. The most recent publications is where the current work is happening. You can see not only what research the professor is currently interested in, but also how frequently the group publishes, who some of the graduate students in the group are (usually the first authors on the papers), and who the group collaborates with (elsewhere in the list of authors on each paper).

Contacting a professor directly is a tried and true way to get your foot in the door. Email is the most common way to get in touch with a professor: it's easy, fast, and doesn't commit you to anything. Those are also reasons why email is the *worst* way to introduce yourself. Around application time, every professor in the department receives dozens of unsolicited emails every day, full of introductory platitudes ("Dear Professor, I would like to introduce myself..."), scripted praise of their work ("I have taken great interest in your recent publications on..."), and pointless questions devised only to elicit a response ("I would appreciate hearing back from you whether..."). They can't be expected to respond to that much random communication, and one can hardly blame them when they don't.

My alternative recommendation: call them on the telephone.

Professors can ignore email, but once they answer their phone, you have their undivided attention. If you have a few conversation topics ready to go, you can get all of the information you want out of the professor while also gaining insight into personality that an impersonal email would never get you. The gumption to pick up the phone puts you leaps and bounds ahead of your other grad-student competitors.

Some professors explicitly warn (for example, on their website) not to contact them. If you want to stay in their good graces, you are advised to respect their wishes, but that doesn't mean you can't get around the problem. One way or another you can get in touch with students or faculty in the department. Those lists of publications should have plenty of grad-student authors, whose contact info is easy to find in an online university directory. Contacting a grad student directly is a sneaky but effective way to get the information you need while not bothering an anti-social professor.

The Application

The grad-school application process is similar to the process of an undergrad application. There's a mountain of paperwork, in which you list every demographic fact about yourself. You'll have to send your undergrad transcripts and GRE scores. The GRE is the "Graduate Record Examination," a test very similar to the SAT which tests your verbal, math, and writing skills and which almost every graduate school requires for admission. For someone heading into grad school in the sciences and engineering, the GRE should not be a challenge, as long as you grab a study guide ahead of time and acclimate yourself to the style of questions. As with all of these sorts of tests, you are usually rewarded more highly for providing the desired or scripted answers than demonstrating any real knowledge. For example, scores on essay sections tend to be positively correlated more to the length of what you write than to actual content. A study guide will tell you explicitly what the test wants you to write.

Several disciplines in the sciences also have subject-specific GREs that are known for being very challenging, and many grad programs for these fields require scores for these exams as well.

Your undergrad program should have resources to prepare you for the subject GRE, and if it doesn't, you should seek it out. Be mindful whether the schools you apply to have a minimum GRE score for consideration of an application. If they do and you don't make the grade, you should save yourself the application fee and look elsewhere, or plan on taking the exam the next time it is offered.

The greatest departure of the grad application from undergrad is the "Statement of Purpose," which may also be called a "Statement of Intent" or something similar. This is a one- or two-page essay, not dissimilar in spirit from a resume cover letter (see Chapter 10), which describes why you want to attend grad school and specifically why their university or department. The application form provides little or no guidance on what to write. The Statement of Purpose is free-form, and it is up to you to make yourself sound like an attractive candidate, where both you and the department will mutually benefit from your presence there.

Although politicians and bureaucrats tout statistics showing that the college-educated population makes substantially more money in a lifetime than those without a bachelor's degree, insinuating in a grad-school Statement of Purpose that you want an *advanced* degree to make more money and ensure still greater financial security is a faux pas of the highest order. For a master's program such an attitude might be forgiven, but not for a Ph.D. An admissions committee is made up of faculty who have devoted their lives to a particular discipline and who are personally invested in academic mission statements, which enshrine the ideas of pedagogical duty and contributing to the knowledge of mankind. Arguing that you want to use a degree to advance your career makes the faculty feel like their knowledge is a commodity to be bought or sold. Regardless of the truth of such a perception, an admissions committee would find it distasteful, and you must therefore pretend that money and career are the furthest things from your mind.

Despite the three "real" reasons for going to grad school, the Statement of Purpose helps you examine in a couple of pages some of your rationale for putting off the real world and staying in school (or, if you're coming from the working world, returning to school). If you can't justify it to yourself now, it will be that much harder a year or two hence when you have to decide on what de-

Tips for Your Statement of Purpose

Do...

    Be specific with inspirational anecdotes

    Identify particular fields and labs that interest you

    Mention what interests you about the university

    Describe communication you had with faculty

Don't...

    Mention the "real" reasons for grad school: inertia, money, and vanity

    Write your autobiography

    Lecture with an in-depth discussion of your field

    Exceed two pages

gree to finish with or what sort of career to pursue. If you avoid naive dreams (e.g., "I want to save the world!" or "I want to win a Nobel Prize!") and assess pragmatic reasons for getting an advanced degree, you'll have the focus to get through your classes and research with a maximum efficiency and far less self-doubt than many of your colleagues.

The strongest trait in an effective Statement of Purpose (for you and for the admissions committee) is specificity. Grand surveys of your life, your family, and your intended field impress no one. The grad school application is the start of the professionalization process. The Statement of Purpose is not the place for an expansive autobiography; instead, include specific anecdotes that motivate your desire to attend grad school. Perhaps you spent summers during undergrad working at an observatory, which inspired you to study astronomy more seriously. Perhaps you volunteered in the prosthetics department of a hospital, which led you to pursue biomedical engineering in grad school. These stories put a personal and well-defined face to the "purpose" part of your Statement of Purpose. They highlight what drives you to pursue a particular field over others and whether a particular department is right for you.

You should also be specific about what you want to do. You have been forced to down-select from biology to genetics, but even within genetics you may need to discuss some subjects or labs that interest you. You'll have to work in a particular lab that studies a very particular corner of the field, and it is important to know what all those corners are. Many departments have a rotation program that lets you sample several labs in your first year of grad school, and discussing these areas of interest in your application shows that you have done your homework and have some understanding of the field that you propose to work in.

You should tailor your Statement to the university you are sending it to. It is tempting to write a one-size-fits-all essay, which saves time, but the lack of seriousness in that sort of writing shows through. A few paragraphs can be uniform (like talking about your anecdotes or motivation), but at some point you have to acknowledge why you want to attend a particular school. If you've looked into this university with any depth, explain why it is a good fit for you. The same goes for the department. Mentioning faculty members by name and your interest in their research makes you appear to have a plan. If you've already been in contact with a professor or two, describe your communication with them thus far and how you hope to continue working with them in the future. The key is to demonstrate a genuine interest in the school and a willingness to go the extra mile.

The Statement of Purpose serves an admissions committee primarily as a signal that you have put at least some thought into your decision to start grad school and into choosing their institution. At some schools it may not count for very much at all. Already having an "in" with a professor is the best way to influence the admissions process (more on that in Chapters 5 and 6). Many schools with graduate programs are large, with dozens (even hundreds) of grad students in each department, and it is impossible to sift through the nuances of every applicant's essay. Many admissions committees rely on your undergrad GPA as the arbiter of acceptance more than anything else. Your Statement of Purpose won't make up for lousy grades, but it may make the difference when it comes to splitting hairs over who gets funding and who doesn't.

The Big Visit

After submitting your application, it goes into the black hole of an admissions committee and you wait, usually several months. In that time, the committee is not only selecting whom they want to accept into their department, but also whom they want to lavish with a visit to the university. The top candidates for a department are invited to visit the school, all expenses paid. From the university's perspective, grad students are valuable for their skilled but very cheap labor. The top candidates will be very productive in their research, help draw new grants to the school, and eventually donate as alumni, but they all get paid a rock-bottom salary as a teaching or research assistant. It's worth dropping a thousand dollars on travel expenses to attract the best students, because on a paltry half-time wage they will generate high-quality conference papers and journal articles, which in turn support hundreds of thousands of dollars in grants.

When you fly to the university, the department has many social and academic events planned for you. You are wined and dined with students and faculty while you get to know the school and the department. There are tours of labs, poster showcases of research, visits to the most impressive sights on campus, guides to the city, and meet-and-greets with other grad students. This is one of the only times you will ever see a university buying and serving alcohol to students. It's a whirlwind of activity, and especially flattering to the ego for someone fresh out of undergrad. The department and the university do everything they can to make their institution appealing.

Now is a good time to meet potential advisors. Before you make the visit, you have to double down on the homework that you did for the application. You're going to meet a lot of people on the visit, and you want to maximize the return on your time there. Find out whose research you have an interest in and seek them out (much more on this in Chapter 3). The visit is the time for *you* to do the interviewing. Although you technically haven't been accepted yet, you're guaranteed to be in. Use your time on campus to interview other grad students and faculty and find out if the fit is right for you.

Your visit to campus is also a visit to the local community. Many large state universities are in rural areas, which may seem like a foreign country if you grew up and spent undergrad in a city. Conversely, grad school in a big city may be overwhelming if you're from a quiet town in the Midwest. The grad students you meet are a prime source of information about the area. You can find out the goings-on about town and also get a feel for how much of a social life they have as grad students. If you are a creature of the night and enjoy partying until dawn, a tiny town in Iowa may not be for you. An avid hiker from the Pacific Northwest may not acclimate well to the flat grid of Manhattan. Nonetheless, every place has more attractions than meet the eye, and first impressions don't necessarily correlate to long-term satisfaction.

Not everyone gets invited to fly in and visit a school, and if you don't get an invitation, you shouldn't let this discourage you. Sometimes the reason is a lack of familiarity. If you are changing your field (say, going from biology to biomedical engineering), an admissions committee may not know what to do with you. You may be a strong candidate, but your transcript only covers undergrad classes for subjects that you would never take or teach in your new department. You may have a lot of basics to learn when you first get to grad school, and the committee may be hesitant to bring you in or offer you funding until you've shown that you have mastered the fundamental material.

Sometimes you simply won't make the cut for a visit. Only a small fraction of the applicants are invited, and not everyone can fit in that exclusive group. That doesn't mean you won't be accepted, it doesn't mean you won't be funded, and it certainly doesn't mean you won't do well in grad school. Not everyone who is funded is invited, and not everyone who is invited accepts, which leaves lots of opportunity to pick up a position. If you have the resources, you can still visit the university on your own, and the department will be happy to show you around. You may not get the ego boost of an all-expenses-paid trip, but your future is still rosy if you know you can succeed. Some of the best test-takers in undergrad—the ones most likely to be courted for visits and funding—crack under the pressure of grad school, which is more about independent motivation and open-ended problem solving. Admissions committees do their best, but faculty members are human, too. There are plenty of ways for them to inadvertently overlook what you have to offer.

The Acceptance Letter

A month or two after the visit (or, in some cases, non-visit), the committee's decision letter arrives in the mail. Your acceptance depends on the same factors that got you into undergrad: grades, your Statement of Purpose, recommendation letters, and the availability of funding.

Some departments guarantee, as a matter of policy, that all of its grad students must be funded (as a teaching or research assistant). In these departments, when they run out of funded slots, they send out rejection letters.

If a department is not bound by such a policy, then nearly everyone with reasonable grades is accepted. Not everyone is funded. The department has nothing to lose by admitting lots of candidates who are not funded: if the candidate chooses not to come, it is no skin off their nose, and if they do enroll, the department gets paid in full. Funding in academia is at historically low levels, which means larger enrollments but fewer funded positions for grad students. If you're not funded, you have several options, which are described in greater detail in Chapter 6.

If your acceptance letter doesn't come with a job offer, that doesn't mean you're sunk, and it doesn't automatically mean you have to take out loans. Making a call to the department's "graduate chair," a faculty member who is in charge of grad-student affairs, yields a lot of useful information about the availability of funding, why you weren't funded, and the likelihood of getting funded in the future. Sometimes there isn't enough money to go around the first year, but a second-year grad student with his or her foot in the door has a much better chance.

Hopefully you have several acceptance letters (and better, several funding offers) to choose from. Make your decision in whatever way satisfies you. Friends and family are a great way to get an objective viewpoint on your problem, but you are the one who has to live with the decision. Your happiness is most important, which is the advice most commonly handed out and the advice most often ignored. If you think you're going to be miserable someplace, then don't go there! If you do, you will spend more time stewing in your own misery than you will working on your research and enjoying a social life. If you swallow a bitter pill because you think you might land some fringe benefits—like a famous name on your diploma or a shiny new lab—you will find yourself only bitterly disappointed.

Chapter 2

Milestones of Grad School

A graduate student's career is marked by a series of tests, separated by months or years of research and study. In the real world, most people measure progress by the passage of time: how many years of experience you have; how long you've been married; how many months until your next dentist appointment. In grad school, students describe the progress of their program in terms of the milestones they've passed, regardless of the time spent between them. One seldom says how many years they've spent in grad school. Rather, you say that you "just passed the quals" or are "about to defend." One grad student may have taken a year before passing the quals, and another may have taken two. No matter, one climbs the grad school hierarchy via these clearly defined stages. The time it took you to pass them is irrelevant.

The process for a master's degrees is supposed to be short and sweet, overseen almost entirely by your advisor. You and your advisor work together to identify a research project that is appropriate for your skills and the degree desired, and your advisor manages your progress over the two years of the project. A master's degree requires fewer forms and less institutional procedure than a Ph.D., and there is less external oversight for your degree. If you write a thesis, your committee (an important group of people discussed later in this chapter) sits in judgment, but your advisor is on the committee as well, to referee. In theory, the committee provides input and guidance for a master's degree, but in practice the committee will contribute no more than you ask of it. The committee members are already too busy with their own Ph.D. students to worry about a research project that may not be finished, probably won't be published, and may be taken up repeatedly by a sequence of master's-degree grad students in the future. If your master's degree is coursework only, the process involves only completing the specified number of credit hours. When you're done with that, you graduate, no questions asked.

The stages of a Ph.D. are more complicated and treacherous, made all the more mystifying by the variety of names that different schools use to identify them. What one school calls a "preliminary exam" another calls the "qualifying exam," and vice versa. One school's "defense" is another school's "prelim" is another's "proposal." Regardless of nomenclature, the same themes appear again and again. There are three milestones for completing your Ph.D.: 1) a test of knowledge in the subject area of your discipline and research, before and after which you are a "Ph.D. student," 2) a presentation and defense of your thesis research plan, after which you become a "Ph.D. candidate," and 3) a defense of your results and conclusions, after which you become the coveted "Ph.D." Not every stage may include an exam, and not every school clearly defines these three stages or treats them all with the same weight.

The Test of Knowledge

The first barrier to entry into the Ph.D. club is academic: a test of your knowledge. If you want to perform research in a field of study, you can't gain admission to the clubhouse until you demonstrate a mastery of the subject material, and this hurdle most commonly takes the form of an exam. A written exam has become the standard, posing several challenging questions in your area of study, sometimes dependent on the curriculum in your department or sometimes more general to the subject matter as a whole. You may also have to take an exam on an ancillary area of study, such as mathematics. The exam may even be tailored to each individual student who takes it, with no two exams exactly alike. It was common in the past for this exam to be oral, or at least in combination with an oral component. In such a scenario, a committee assigns you a handful of questions, which you may or may

The Milestones of the Ph.D.

Milestone	Takes the Form...	Called...
1. Test of technical knowledge	Written exam *or* Oral exam *or* Written report	"Quals" "Qualifying Exam" "Prelim" "Preliminary Exam" "Exams"
	⬇	
2. Research proposal	Written proposal *and* Oral presentation	"Quals" "Qualifying Exam" "Prelim" "Preliminary Exam" "General Exam" "Proposal" "Defense"
	⬇	
3. Defense of completed research	Written dissertation *and* Oral defense	"Defense" "Dissertation Defense" "Thesis Defense"

not be allowed to review beforehand, and you are expected to answer them on a blackboard while the committee peppers you with questions.

At many universities this examination serves as a filter for the committed and qualified grad students and is not to be taken lightly. You may need to spend an entire semester preparing for this exam, at the expense of classes and research. The test of knowledge is a test of your commitment to your degree program. If you can't make the effort to internalize the subject material, you won't be expected to survive the rigors of peer review and a dissertation defense. Therefore, this stage functions as a weeding-out phase for many departments, and you only get one or two tries before you are simply asked to leave. Although you may feel confident in your mastery of the material, you are well-served to know exactly how challenging your examination will be. If you don't take it seriously—a frequent pitfall among over-confident grad students—you may regret it and spend more than a semester making up for lost time.

Not all departments require these time- and cram-intensive exams any more. Some have done away with them entirely, reasoning that if you can complete research in the field you presumably must also have sufficient knowledge of the field (in addition to the classes you must attend). Other departments have focused this test of knowledge to your specific research area by assigning a written report. A report-based test of your knowledge involves, for example, preparing a review article of all the published research to date in your area. Preparation of such a twenty- or thirty-page document, with its fifty or hundred references, thoroughly prepares you to enter the arena of cutting edge research, possibly even more so than if you had regurgitated textbook knowledge in a traditional written or oral exam.

The Research Proposal

In the second stage of the Ph.D., you define your research. The first year or two of grad school is spent getting to know the field, doing experiments, and building a picture in your mind of where you fit into the field and how you want to contribute. In consultation with your advisor, you build a research plan for the rest of your degree and take it to your committee for approval. In this examination, you are asking the committee, "This is what I think is enough for my Ph.D. Do you agree?" If they do, you move boldly into the no-man's land of a grad career, where there are no more demands or hurdles but for your defense.

This research proposal contains two elements: a written document and a presentation. The written proposal is tens of pages long, depending on limits imposed by your department, and outlines the plan for your Ph.D. The proposal has two distinct parts: what you've already done, and what you plan to do. For those who have already completed a large amount of research, your proposal document might contain nearly all of your dissertation material already. It may also include a literature review, which serves as a survey and introduction to your research and demonstrates to your committee that you are familiar with the latest work of your peers.

Your proposal's first objective is to highlight the research that you've already done. In addition to exams and classes, you perform an enormous amount of research before you even begin to formulate your official research proposal. A description of the work you've already done demonstrates that you have the competence to carry out research, that you are familiar with the methods of your field, and that you are committed to this process of finishing your degree. Your research must not only contribute to your field, you must also be able to accomplish it in a few years with a reasonable chance of success. Just figuring out what is achievable takes two or more years of work in a lab. In that time, you may have produced a number of exciting results already. You may have been to a few conferences and even published a journal article or two. The more experience you have under your belt, the easier it is to propose the last details of your research as a plan, and the easier it is for your committee to pass you.

Having established your credibility as a researcher, you secondly propose your plan of action to complete your dissertation. If you demonstrate a competent grasp of your research and its place in the field, you can spell out what points remain to call your project done. The research tasks that you list in this "to do" category flow naturally from the work you've already accomplished, so that the committee knows you are in a strong position to complete them. If you were to propose taking on a different research project entirely for the rest of your Ph.D., the committee might wonder how you expect to tackle new material effectively after you've invested so much time in another project.

These future research plans should be thorough and exhaustive. This doesn't mean you have to accomplish every goal you lay out for the committee, but it is better that you propose too much work than too little. If your proposal looks thin, the committee may take it upon itself to suggest additional experiments and investigations, by which they mean they *demand* that you follow up on their suggestions.

You present this proposal to your committee in person, accompanied by an oral presentation. Odds are that no one on your committee has actually read the proposal cover to cover. Your presentation is probably the only thing standing between you and becoming a Ph.D. candidate, so you must not leave out anything important and assume that the "rest" is covered in the proposal itself. You should spell out clearly what you've done and what you plan to do, as in the written document, but the oral presentation is an opportunity to provide more informal commentary. You can demonstrate why your research matters and where it stands in respect to the rest of the literature. The proposal is not the time to instruct the committee on your research, but rather to be clear why your research is worthy of a Ph.D.

Your university or department probably has rules regarding when you submit your proposal to the committee, and a few weeks before the presentation is a typical deadline for your written proposal. This gives your committee ample time to skim the first few pages, forget about it for three weeks, and then skim the same pages again a few minutes before your presentation. In addition to your proposal document, you should prepare a package for each committee member that contains hard copies of your other relevant academic accomplishments, such as journal articles or conference papers. This extra heft demonstrates how you are making an effort at taking part in the research community. They won't read these either, but they might look at the titles and the names of the journals and conferences.

Your research proposal is not a contract. After preparing a long list of future "to do" items and after your committee passes you, you might feel obligated to actually do everything you said you would. Unless an item is absolutely necessary for the defense of your thesis, this is not the case. Your proposal is packed with research ideas to show the committee that you know what you're doing and comprehend the breadth of your field, but you cannot be expected to accomplish everything. In the course of your subsequent research, you may find that some of your proposed avenues were dead ends or that their benefit was outweighed by the time investment. You are free to push some research items aside.

The Defense

The grand finale of your grad career is the defense of your dissertation (or, master's thesis). At your defense, you throw everything you have at your committee and defend the results of your research. Ideally, you demonstrate that your thesis and conclusions are supported by the results you have, bolstered by journal articles you have published and by any other professional accomplishments that swing in your favor. The defense itself, which is an oral presentation, comes a few weeks after submitting your written dissertation, which has about as little chance of being read as your proposal. This presentation is your big moment. All or part of the defense may be open to the public, where you can invite family and friends to cheer you on while you are grilled by four extremely bored professors.

Your defense is above all about *you* and *your* contributions. This is not an instructional seminar on your subject material. No matter who is in the audience, this defense is for your committee, and you can assume that its members have the technical background to judge your research. If they have a question, they'll ask. It is not your job to figure out what the committee members don't know. You're there to show off your research and to make it stand out in relief against the rest of the field. This is no time to be modest, and no time to talk about how "we" did any research, the way you would in a journal article. You are free to use the first person singular and talk about what "I" did. The presentation should make it very clear the research questions you asked, what your results are, and how they support your conclusions. Ultimately, you need to answer for the committee a very simple question: "What do we know now that we didn't know before?"

If your formal presentation occurs in front of an audience of friends and family, the committee may not really grill you, lest they look mean-spirited. When you're done, the audience is asked to leave so you can get down to business. In a closed session—if there is one—the examining faculty have the chance to be frank. They might have expressed mild skepticism about a point with an audience in the room, but they may take you to task behind closed doors. High-level give-and-take with the committee probes the foundations of your research, the veracity of your conclusions, and the conviction with which you defend them. The committee is *not* looking for a reason to fail you. They want you to succeed. If you show them the depth of your understanding and take their critique in good cheer, you will be fine.

When the committee is done with you, you are dismissed and they confer. The committee deliberates alone for ten or fifteen minutes, but the question of passing your defense is usually settled in the first two. The rest of the time is spent by the faculty filling out forms for the registrar and chit-chatting about the weather. There is seldom any question about a Ph.D. candidate passing his or her defense. If your advisor does his job even remotely competently, he won't let you defend unless you're going to pass. In truth, the defense is mostly a formality. After years of scrutiny from your advisor, defending a research proposal, presenting research to skeptical colleagues at conferences, and fending off hostile reviewers for your journal articles, the committee at your defense is really just more of the same criticism you've been dealing with for years. This doesn't mean you won't be nervous. The defense is not a cakewalk, but failing a Ph.D. defense is exceedingly unusual. Most professors can count on one hand the number of defense failures they've witnessed, and most of those can be chocked up to an inattentive advisor letting his student defend before he or she was ready.

After the committee finishes the paperwork, they emerge from their chamber with a handshake, a smile, and light banter of congratulations. In addition to the signed forms, you might be handed a few conditions before you've officially passed. In the worst case, the committee is on the fence in terms of your having completed all of your work. They might send you back to your word processor to re-work some of your conclusions. You may have to make some edits to your thesis here and there where the committee felt changes are necessary. They may also impose some unique conditions, like requiring that you submit all of your journal-article manuscripts before graduation. Regardless, when you have those forms in hand, you're home free. The extra work they might tack on is child's play compared to everything else that came before.

The three phases of your Ph.D. (a test of knowledge, scrutiny of your research plan, and defense) carry different weights depending on the university you attend and the department you work in. Where I went to graduate school, the knowledge examination was very challenging, requiring a full semester of preparation, and served as a weeding-out process for those not serious about the Ph.D. program, whereas the presentation of the research plan was a straightforward process that few if any failed. On the other hand, my friends in another department had to write a review article for their knowledge test, which nearly everyone passed, but the research proposal was the stage where grad students more often stumbled. As you embark on your time in grad school, you will learn where your own department stands on this scale. You can learn the most by asking students who are further on or nearing the end of their program. They will give you an unvarnished assessment of the department's demands. The professors themselves will more likely insist that all of the examinations are equally important and challenging, which may be ideal but does not reflect reality.

For all the work preparing for your defense and other examinations, you may find the most stress lies not in the examination itself but in your utter helplessness to schedule them. Your committee members are busy people, and a herculean effort is called for to get four or five of them in the same room at the same time for an hour or more. The committee's schedule is so packed you won't really have a choice when the exam actually occurs. If you try to schedule too early in the semester, inevitably one or two committee members won't fully commit because you're asking too early. If you wait until too late in the semester, the professors complain about how tight their schedules are and that you gave them so little notice. You'll spend two or three days iterating between four different schedules that you have no control over, hoping and praying that a two-hour slot is free for everyone three weeks hence. When the time comes for your exam, you'll fret less about the exam and more about making sure that all of your committee shows up.

Your Committee

The formal judges of your entrance into the academic brotherhood of the M.S. or Ph.D. are your committee, a panel of three to five Ph.D.'s, usually faculty, who serve at your request as mentors and who ultimately hold the keys to your graduation. Your committee approves your research plan, administers the preliminary examination for your research proposal, and sits in judgment at your final defense. The committee is a voice that represents the "community" and determines whether you have completed the requirements to achieve a degree. The committee also serves the practical purpose of ensuring that your advisor alone cannot manipulate the system to get his students an advanced degree. Without this oversight, advisors may be tempted to compromise standards and move students out as quickly as possible, or to graduate students who are not ready.

Your committee arguably serves its most useful purpose during the preparation and defense of your research plan. Up to that point, your committee has functioned as a list of names on a form, satisfying bureaucratic requirements. When they come together to inspect your plan, the committee members have the opportunity to provide input that even your advisor may not foresee. Four or five experienced minds in the same room offer a valuable opportunity to discover new avenues of research and identify pitfalls that you hadn't considered for your proposed work.

Many grad students approach the preliminary exam with a confrontational attitude, prepared to defend their research plan against an onslaught of skepticism. The committee is no doubt a skeptical body, but they are not only looking for reasons your project could fail. They want to put at your disposal every intellectual weapon they have to bring your research closer to success, and your own advisor doesn't have them all. The members of your committee observe your research each from their own personal angle, which can only improve your final product. If you prepare the defense of your research plan as a collaborative event, your experience will be far less stressful.

Your committee also sits in judgment at your defense, but it mostly functions as a rubber stamp. If your advisor is a competent and respected member of the faculty, a committee approves whatever the advisor wants (namely, passing you). The committee may not go easy on you, but it is exceptionally rare that the final outcome is in question. The committee probes the depth of your knowledge and research, but they are not trying to ruin you. After they've given you the third degree, you get the stamp of approval.

Except for the most egregious cases, a committee doesn't dare fail a student, which would likely spark a faculty civil war within the department. Committees are incestuous. Professors regularly sit on the committees of their colleagues' students, and failing a colleague's grad student almost certainly would lead to the same treatment when the roles are reversed. The system would break down if committees were truly independent and unbiased evaluators. Instead, the committee functions as an acquiescent politburo for you and your advisor.

The role of the committee, however, is not nearly as important as who is on it. At almost every university, your advisor is the chair of the committee, and his presence is essential. He has followed everything you've done as a grad student, he probably wrote the grants, and he may have designed some of the methodology himself before you came along. If your research involves an unorthodox approach, you may not have the gravitas as a young professional to argue the finer points, whereas your advisor has the reputation and experience that can soothe the concerns of a skeptical committee. Your advisor likely knows everyone on the committee and has been through many examinations and defenses with them before. He knows the questions each professor likes to ask and the probable areas of confusion for each professor. In sticky situations, a few words from your advisor can clarify a point that would take you ten minutes to explain. However, in general the role of committee chair is titular. The chair supposedly controls the proceedings of your examinations, but the events themselves are so informal in practice that his role has little substantive difference from the rest of the committee members.

Your committee is composed of Ph.D.'s, primarily faculty, but not all necessarily from your department. The only prerequisite, aside from a Ph.D., is some technical background that applies to your research. A physics professor would be entirely appropriate on a mechanical engineering committee, or a chemist on a biology committee. At least one faculty member must sit on your committee, because the university is responsible for the conferral of your degree, but it is also possible to have other Ph.D.'s on your committee. You may bring a distinguished Ph.D. from industry to sit on your committee, especially if your research was funded by that researcher's employer. These adjunct committee members don't make up the "core" of your committee, but they can be helpful over the course of your research and during the development of your research plan.

Most grad students are allowed to choose the makeup of their committee. When the time comes to assemble one, you approach each professor in person and humbly request that they serve on your committee, and they nearly always say yes. However, you shouldn't ask just anybody to serve on your committee. The selection process must be strategic to ensure both your long-term success as a grad student and minimal hassle.

The path of least resistance is to find as many professors as possible who are guaranteed rubber stamps. These committee members are qualified technically to sit on your committee but may not have enough knowledge of your particular field to pick you apart. They provide valuable insight because of their different perspective, but they won't come down too hard on you, because they know the limits of their expertise.

Career advancers are another strategic choice for your committee. If you snag a big name for your committee, you might pick up extra caché on your resume. The well connected big name can also help with finding a post-doctoral position or a job when you've finished your grad program.

If you exhaust rubber-stamp and big-name candidates, your best bet is to find professors who like you. However, there may be obligatory members of your committee besides your advisor. If your research area has only two professors at the university, then that other faculty member almost certainly must sit on the committee. Whether you want that professor on your committee or not is overshadowed by the courtesy appointment, which is necessary to keep peace in the department.

You should avoid committee members who don't like you, obviously, and those who don't like your advisor, which is not so obvious. Your advisor and the faculty are humans, too. They are subject to the same petty bigotry and closed-mindedness of all mere mortals, which means your advisor may have academic enemies, even within the department. If your advisor likes to make waves, is very outspoken, or frequently battles with faculty over research philosophy, there may be cliques of professors who don't get along, and these are not the people to have on your committee. Over the years as a grad student, you will identify these camps, and you should take care not to endanger your own well being by dragging them together onto a committee. It is better to let them fight their battles at faculty meetings, where the stakes are low, than to be caught in the crossfire at your defense.

Your Thesis

Your thesis is a sacred document, the culmination of a half-decade of hard work during which you transformed into a professional scientist or engineer. Your thesis is also a brick of paper bound together with shaky assumptions, massaged data, and unaddressed problems dressed up as "future work." After several years of slaving away, you will have built up a solid body of accomplishment, but you know better than anybody where the holes are. There are spots where you know you could have done a few extra experiments, run some more permutations, and tightened up the statistics, but the demands of your advisor, journal article reviewers, and your committee make the perfect thesis document impossible. What does matter is creating a corpus that can stand up soundly to peer review, warts notwithstanding.

Your thesis condenses the last several years of your life into one book, which looks so tiny in comparison to the effort expended to produce it. The length of a thesis, whether M.S. or Ph.D., varies widely from person to person and across fields. A mathematics Ph.D. can be as short as 30–50 pages (proofs don't take up a lot of space), whereas computer-science theses can go on for hundreds of pages. Your department probably has a library of its own with all of its archived theses going back a few decades. If you can access it, survey the thesis landscape and guesstimate what thesis length is appropriate. You'll probably find that between 100 and 200 pages is common, with the occasional outliers on the thin and thick sides. The objective of your thesis is to say what you need to say and nothing more. You present your research, state and support your conclusions, and call it a day. If it only takes you 75 pages to do that properly, then you have a 75 page thesis. No one benefits—neither you doing the writing nor your committee doing the reading—if you inflate the page count with unnecessary verbiage.

Each thesis is as unique as its creator, and trying to universally cover what "goes into" a thesis will satisfy no one. With your long record of research to rely on, you will have no shortage of things to say, and how you want to say it is up to you. Breaking up your thesis into appropriate chapters, whether by topic or by chronology, depends on the special circumstances associated with your research. My thesis had two distinct and unrelated sections, each broken up into their own chapters. I have seen theses that went step by step from introduction to methodology to results to discussion to conclusions, like an overgrown lab report. Thesis writing is one of those key moments where your advisor advises you. Get his input on what he likes in his students' theses and what he thinks is appropriate for you. There are, however, a handful of items that appear in every thesis but receive less attention than they deserve.

Prefatory material is the part of your thesis that is very important by tradition but that few ever receive guidance on. This material includes your dedication, abstract, and acknowledgments. The dedication you may do with as you please; parents, spouses, and children are common recipients. The thesis abstract is similar to a journal-article abstract, only on a larger scale. In the abstract, you attempt to condense your entire thesis into a single page, not more than a paragraph or two, that keeps to the facts and emphasizes the impact of your work. The abstract may be the only part of your thesis that a committee member (or posterity) reads.

The acknowledgments page has a few pro forma requirements. Obviously, your advisor comes first and foremost. He's been there through thick and thin, and this is the one spot where you can show your appreciation. Friends and colleagues may warrant a shout out as well. You *must* also include an acknowledgment to your committee, thanking them for their time and their guidance. You may have never consulted with your committee over the last five years—nor used any more of their time than two hours for your research proposal and defense—but they still get acknowledged as if they had been advising you for years on enterprises of great pitch and moment. It's just the way it is.

You must discuss the subject matter of your thesis with an introduction chapter of some kind, but keep in mind that you are not writing a textbook. It is tempting to pen a long exegesis of your field, starting with quotes from Pythagoras and leading up to the present day, summing up the corpus of human achievement in your tiny corner of the world once and for all. If you have months to spare on a long and torturous exposition of material that your readers already know and that has no bearing on acquiring your degree, go right ahead. The smart money, however, is on the grad student who offloads as much history as possible to an exhaustive list of references, with only the minimum background included to explain the context of your research and the symbols in your math, and to demonstrate that you know something about the bigger picture. You can leave the bloated exposition to that day when you're a tenured professor penning your magnum opus.

Your thesis must get through your committee on its content, and through the bureaucracy on its formatting. Everything else is gravy. Don't beat yourself up over it, and don't fret if you haven't produced the next *Principia*. A common method of thesis construction involves little to no writing at all: if you already have several conference papers, journal articles, and other written material (including your old research proposal), you can create the classic Frankenstein thesis. Strip out the introductions from your papers and call the remainder of each a chapter, and you have most of a dissertation right there. All of the introductions can be cobbled together into an introductory chapter, and all you have left to write is a chapter on your future work. You still have to make the thesis a coherent document, but the Frankenstein method saves a lot of time. If you don't have a large corpus to fall back on, you're stuck doing a lot of writing. Even so, the publishing process should come after the thesis is out the door. If you try to make every chapter of your thesis a publishable paper, you can't expect to graduate on time. Get the thesis done, and then do the refinements for publication in your own good time.

When you're writing your thesis, it's important to hold your literary urges in check. It is a great achievement to compose a thesis, but no one is going to read it. Your advisor will peruse it, fix your typos, and police your conclusions; your committee may skim it or read the first chapter or two. But you will agonize over it. And yet, after you defend, you will seldom if ever look at it again. Your thesis will become a trophy on a shelf in your office, gathering esteemed dust. You'll send copies to your parents and relatives, but they won't understand it. New grad students following in your footsteps may crack it open, but everything worth studying or repeating is already in your conference papers, posters, and journal articles. There is no need to lose sleep or precious weeks worrying whether your composition would pass muster by Hemingway or Dickens.

Graduating

Knowing about the hurdles and milestones of grad school is one thing, but how are you supposed to know when you're ready for each one? After years of research, conferences, and publications, how do you know when it's finally time to graduate?

You are intimately familiar with the demands imposed by the bureaucracy to achieve your desired degree. A fixed number of credit hours are required as a baseline to graduate. These numbers are usually set by a higher entity in the university, not by the department, and they specify not only the number of hours to complete, but also the kinds of classes you have to take.

Forms are the food that feeds the bureaucratic leviathan. If you need to do anything relating to the school, especially in an official capacity regarding your degree, you have to fill out a form, or two, or three. There's a form to fill out when you matriculate, when you want to register for classes, when you prepare for quals or prelims or your defense. If you're lucky, the university lets you fill out these forms online. Regardless, you submit the forms and they enter the "system," probably never to be seen again. There's no telling what the purpose of the forms is, or where they go, but your degree is made or broken by the them.

Although the bureaucracy has established oppressive rules and guidelines, thankfully they are clearly defined and achievable. Credit hours can be counted, summed, and checked off the list of graduation requirements. Exams can be taken, and passing grades assigned. However, there are unwritten rules that come along with graduation. No one writes them down, and they have no uniform definition. Nonetheless, living up to subjective guidelines are just as important as submitting your forms on time.

For a master's degree, most of the hurdles to graduation are time- and bureaucracy-based. If you take the classes and submit the forms, you're most of the way there. If you're doing a coursework-only master's, you're all of the way there. For a thesis master's, you write up a document with some original work. You present and defend your work, but what exactly must be in this work is ambiguously defined. A master's degree is a far cry from a Ph.D. You're not usually expected to make a "major" contribution to your field through publications and conferences, although your own advisor may require it to varying degrees. A master's thesis can be as simple as implementing a new computer program, reproducing the results of a previous researcher, or carrying out a straightforward sequence of experiments.

Some schools and departments have a very high bar for master's degrees, especially if they usually don't issue them. In the sciences, one usually goes straight from undergraduate to a Ph.D. program, so a master's degree is an anomalous consolation prize that the department sets a high standard for. You may not have done as much work as a Ph.D., but you still must have solid results and defend your work in front of a skeptical committee. In engineering, you typically have to go through a complete master's program before you can continue on to a Ph.D., in which case a master's thesis may have nearly as much work as a Ph.D. on its own.

For a Ph.D., the real requirement for graduation is easily defined but ambiguously accomplished: "contribute" to your field. The line between the research you do for a master's thesis and a contribution worthy of a Ph.D. is hazy, and one could argue that a Ph.D. merely constitutes more in volume than a master's degree. The yardstick that directly measures the contribution of your Ph.D. is publication of articles in a peer-reviewed journal. Without those publications (or, completed work that your committee deems publishable), graduation is in doubt. Attendance at conferences, where you meet new colleagues and build a professional network, bolsters the argument that you've contributed to the field, but conferences are only the window dressing. Publications are your ticket out of grad school.

Your advisor is an indispensable guide on the way to defining your contribution and its sufficiency for graduation. Over the course of your graduate career, you will not only work on your own research but also watch the progress of others. Friends and colleagues ahead of you will finish their own degrees, and you will attend many defenses, if they're open to the public. You will get the gist of this contribution requirement by osmosis, so that by the time you are ready to graduate, you'll feel that you are ready yourself. You'll see how the work you've done compares to those who have come before and assess whether it is time for you to move on as well. If you feel unsure or underprepared to defend a Ph.D., then it *is* too early.

In the film *Full Metal Jacket*, the protagonist, James "Joker"

Davis, narrates a scene at the end of boot camp: "Graduation is only a few days away and the recruits of platoon thirty-ninety-two are salty...The drill instructors are proud to see that we are growing beyond their control. The Marine Corps does not want robots." These enlisted men had entered boot camp as rowdy boys, lacking discipline and direction, and the military was happy to provide structure in their lives before sending them off to war. The men were trained to follow every order of their drill instructor without question, no matter how ridiculous. Training was arduous, baffling, and at times humiliating, and after a few months of instruction, the Marine Corps had trained the platoon to be soldiers. These marines, however, were not unthinking automatons. The drill instructors had taught them to take initiative, so that they no longer needed verbal abuse to do what was necessary. The hovering instructors eventually became an aggravation, even a hindrance, to getting the job done. Simply surviving thirteen weeks of boot camp was not the sign that they were ready to graduate. Pushing back against the instructors and growing into individual soldiers beyond their control was.

Most students in technical fields start grad school fresh out of, or shortly after, undergrad. The professor, who is now your advisor, still has an aura about him, and not knowing the first thing about doing research, you rely on him for direction. Your goal is an advanced degree, and your advisor is the closest contact you have who can lead you to that golden ticket. Your advisor (or, perhaps, an experienced post-doc) supervises your first lab experiments, your first conference, and your first journal article. You depend on your advisor to induct you into this academic brotherhood.

After a few years, though, you've learned the ropes inside and out. You've seen your advisor's strengths and weaknesses, and you start to have your own ideas about how to do your research. You chafe under the very advice you used to rely on. You become more outspoken in group meetings, you ask fewer questions, and you start to ignore some of his advice because you know your work now better than he does.

Being ready to graduate from grad school is not a function of time. An M.S. can take a year or two, a Ph.D. can take four or six or ten. Students who take more time than others do not necessarily have "better" results, nor are they more devoted to their work. Students who take less time are not "smarter" or "luckier." For your entire life up through undergrad, academic advancement occurred on a chronological basis. Every year you moved on to a new set of classes. After four years of high school, you graduated. After four (or, these days, five) years of college, you graduated. Getting out of grad school is not about time. It's about becoming a professional, and that process knows no clock. Your advisor won't need to tell you when to graduate. You will know when you are ready, probably before he does. You realize that you not only don't need your advisor any more, you don't want him.

Chapter 3

Your Advisor

Your undergraduate curriculum was much broader than anything you encounter in advanced study. In grad school, you develop a specialization, an area of expertise. You build the unique resume that someone will eventually pay you for. Undergrad was about hitting the books and getting educated, but grad school finally puts into practice the material you learned in undergrad. By doing, grad school shapes you into a *professional*. The practice of a field of study cannot be taught solely on paper. Formulae go into textbooks and procedures into manuals, but the sixth sense of knowing bad data from ugly data or sensing that you've overlooked a critical assumption comes only with experience and through trial and error. Honing such practical but ineffable skills requires hands-on guidance, and this is where your advisor comes in.

Your advisor is your boss and your mentor. He pays your bills, and he illuminates the path towards your M.S. or Ph.D.* He is the man with the benefit of experience and hindsight. He won't hold your hand the whole way through your advanced degree, but he can steer you onto the right path so that, with any luck, you graduate in a timely fashion.

The quality of the relationship with your advisor dramatically affects the quality of your grad school experience, and choosing an

---

*Given the high frequency with which the advisor is referred to in the third person, the politically correct but lengthy "he or she" is simply too cumbersome. In a politically incorrect spirit, I have chosen to use "he."

advisor may be more momentous than even choosing the school itself. This chapter provides some insight into who your advisor is, what his job is, how you can acquire an advisor, and how to survive working closely with this person for several years.

Who is Your Advisor?

Your advisor is many things, but above all he is a regular person. Universities and their faculty cultivate an aura of wisdom and even infallibility around professors. During the undergraduate experience, instructors have all the answers by design. Cracks in the façade may begin to show towards the end of college, but there's always one way or another to get the right answers on homework and exams and to please the wise man with the answer sheet. As you enter graduate school, you interact with this professor—now your advisor—on a peer-like level. He is still your superior, and he has more experience, but he won't have all the answers, and his individual quirks as a person shine brightly in contrast to the controlled image that prevails in class.

Your advisor is himself a former graduate student, and he too had an advisor. He has been through the same challenges of research and bureaucracy in grad school that you face, and he knows how challenging they are. In all likelihood, he has led many other students through this process already, but how your advisor wields the benefit of his experience depends on the individual. Some may simply not care; professors, as in most professions, are a cross-section of humanity, and there are always some people who cannot be bothered with other people's problems (regardless of the fact that it's in their job description). Other advisors may view the confusing rituals of grad school as a rite of passage and leave you to muddle through it the way they did. Some advisors are mindful of their students' sanity and try to keep tabs on your psychological state.

As you look at the faculty demographics of your own grad school, you will see a league of nations represented. In many disciplines, academia is the only opportunity for employment in the United States, and some nations lack the industry to support individuals with advanced degrees. For example, Venezuela has little by way of an aerospace industry, and a Venezuelan grad student in aerospace engineering has little choice but to remain in the United States to pursue that field as a career. But for such fields so closely related to national security, often only United States citizens can be hired in industry, and academia becomes the only option.

Working with a foreign advisor requires an adjustment period as you reach a social equilibrium. Faculty from outside the United States may have drastically different expectations in every aspect of your performance as a grad student. Expectations of how much you will work, how much you *should* work, and how much he is responsible for as an advisor can differ greatly from American faculty. Even subtle aspects of interaction, such as how respect is shown, become points of culture shock. A Japanese advisor may show, receive, and expect deference in a different fashion from an Argentinian. Working with foreign faculty in most respects will be the same as with anyone else, but it is wise to keep in mind that an extra adjustment period may be necessary.

Your advisor is a researcher. Why else would he have become a professor? Your advisor does research because he loves it. For someone in academia, research is more than a job, it is a calling. It is something your advisor lives and breathes. He thinks about it all the time. An interesting problem can keep him up at night, and new questions and problems bubble up around him at any moment. Being not just his job but his passion, research is something that he *must* do. Some men love their cars, others love sports. Your advisor loves his research, and it is the primary reason he became a professor.

Your advisor is also a teacher. In theory, teaching is the primary responsibility of a university professor, and a large chunk of his time is spent preparing for and leading his classes. Your advisor may view the teaching aspect of his job as a joy or an evil. Some professors enjoy teaching and devote great effort to it. I have known university instructors who spend two hours before every lecture studying their notes, or who personally grade every homework assignment, or who show up to late-night homework group sessions in the common room to help their students out. Other professors loathe teaching in its entirety, put minimal effort into classes, and have teaching assistants take on as much load as they can bear. As an undergraduate you no doubt identified this type, and wise students avoid them wherever possible.

Lastly, a fact often overlooked: your advisor is an employee of the university. Your advisor's teaching load depends on his tenure level. Assistant professors, especially the newest tenure-track hires, teach several classes per semester (possibly three or more). They teach introductory classes, a frustrating and thankless job that few of the senior faculty want. The assistant professors simultaneously try to create new advanced classes in their area of research, as part of the road to tenure. Associate professors, who are tenured, have a lighter teaching load, but may still teach two classes per semester. They get to shy away from the introductory classes and teach higher-level material. The full professors and most senior faculty have a similar load, but they may get to pick and choose their classes, rather than be assigned them, or they may not have to teach at all. Teaching load also depends on funding. It is not uncommon for a tenured professor to "buy" his way out of teaching with research dollars directed to the department.

Your Advisor's Job

Many people enter graduate school with the expectation of being guided from beginning to end by their advisor and executing the professors' orders as part of a research program. This is not the way grad school works. *You* are the one doing *your* research. The department accepted your application based in part on your Statement of Purpose, in which you described the kind of research that you want to carry out. Although a professor may pay you from research grants as part of a larger project, what you do with those funds within that project is your responsibility. The professor does not have a rote plan for students to complete an M.S. or Ph.D. There are no rules. You are there to perform research that a committee of faculty approves. Your advisor's job is to guide you to the point where you can defend your work before those peers and enter the world as a professional scientist or engineer.

Advising on research begins well before the research itself. Choosing a topic for your research can take a year or more of searching and dabbling before a solid idea begins to form. Once you've identified a research topic, your advisor guides you on how to approach the problem. There are many right ways to solve a research problem, and there are many wrong ways. He helps sift through the options. He can also judge whether the problem you've selected is soluble at all. Many grad students in the 19th and 20th centuries no doubt hoped to solve Fermat's last theorem, and hopefully their advisors steered them away from that intractable problem, which wasn't solved until 1995 (and not by a grad student).

Your advisor cannot dictate your personal style of doing research, but he can step in when you get down to specifics. Your research will generate enormous amounts of data, and in your early years you may have no idea what to do with it or what it means. Your advisor provides guidance on where to go with your results, and whether the conclusions you've drawn really are supported by the data. Over time you'll gain experience to do this job yourself, but at the beginning you may not know what to do. In fact, in your particular research you may eventually excel beyond your advisor, who juggles multiple projects simultaneously.

Your advisor also helps frame the message of the research. It can be hard to keep perspective after being sequestered in your lab for months. Research tends to be done out of order, following a growing network of paths and tangents, without an obvious outcome waiting for you. Going from one result or experiment to the next, sometimes the message is lost, and you can lose sight of what you're really looking to demonstrate with your work. The big picture suffers, but the big picture is what your advisor depends on to get that next grant. Sometimes you go down one branch of research, hit a wall, and become depressed by the lack of progress. Your advisor can point out that such a fruitless branch wasn't even really the point of the research, and careful message-control in your publications can avoid the roadblock all together. Alternatively, your advisor may have just the impartial perspective you need to demonstrate that your work wasn't so fruitless after all.

Beyond the practical guidance in day-to-day research, your advisor is expected to advise on your degree program as a whole. Your advisor can tell you if a research problem is soluble, and he can also gauge whether the problem is sufficient for an M.S. or Ph.D., and whether it can be completed in a timely fashion. Experience develops an eye to identify the subjective dividing line between what is and isn't enough to graduate. Unfortunate grad students without proper oversight may stumble into the trap of reproducing someone else's work or adding only a nominal amount of scholarship to an extant corpus. An attentive advisor makes sure that you don't learn about such inadequacies while you're on the spot during your defense, when there's no turning back.

Academics is an area where your advisor may or may not feel obligated to comment. There are classes you must take to graduate, but the wide range of electives can significantly impact the progress of your research. You and your advisor should discuss every semester during registration which classes appear the most relevant to your work or round out your base of experience. You may find that some classes, although part of your area of expertise, are not necessary because you teach yourself. Just getting started in research requires a lot of catching up on material that was never covered in undergrad, and you may find that by the time you have the opportunity to take certain classes, they have nothing new to offer.

You also need to determine when your advisor expects you to be done with classes. Under most circumstances, your class load in grad school is completed in the first two or three years. The rest of your time is devoted to work in the lab. You don't want to overwork yourself with classes, but if you choose too light a load, you may find yourself still dealing with homework and lectures several years into your program, when you should be devoting nearly all of your time to research. You want to develop a plan with your advisor that gets you all of the educational value you need while still getting your research done punctually.

Types of Advisors

There are as many types of advisors as there are people. Each has his own quirks, faults, vices, fancies, and habits. However, life in academia tends to attract a certain sort of individual, and the pace of life in the ivory tower molds personalities differently from life in the outside world. The medieval, authoritarian structure of academia reinforces these personalities, because no serfs (the students) dare speak up against professors' obnoxious habits, and academia itself insulates its members from negative consequences when such traits develop. After spending some time in grad school you will pick up the main themes of personality in the faculty. Some of it depends on the person involved, and some on the stage of the academic's career. This section lists the major classifications that you will encounter. A real advisor is a combination of these characters, but frequently one or two particular characters dominate. Don't let these caricatures get you down: all advisors have plenty of good traits, too, but it's the eccentricities that stick in your memory and that you will spend most of your time griping about with your friends.

1. **The Control Freak.** This advisor subjects his group to a reign of terror. The control freak has to be right all of the time, thanks to an inflated sense of himself and his accomplishments, which may actually be considerable. He never admits to an error, and to those who point out his occasional gaffe, no matter how minor, he responds with passive-aggressive pique, shunning the offenders in group meetings or criticizing them in public.

   The control freak must have his hands in everything you do. He is a micro-manager who knows how to do everything better than the way you plan on doing it, even though he hasn't done the work himself in decades. Demanding to have a hand in every aspect of your research spills over into your publications, where he may insist on being the first author for nearly everything.

   The control freak maintains an intimidating reputation not only at the university, but also among his peers and colleagues. Then why do students work for him? His intense and perfectionist personality has likely garnered him substantial grant money. A career of well-funded research has led to success and accolades that, in turn, generate acolytes.

2. **The Tenure Seeker.** The tenure seeker is a young faculty member—an assistant professor—on a quest for the brass ring of tenure. Tenure, the holy grail for every academic, is a contractual right conferred by a university that prohibits the tenure-holder's termination without just cause. That is, if an individual is tenured, he or she is free to say and do just about anything they want provided that they don't commit a crime and that they live up to their other contractual obligations, such as teaching and committee requirements, which are usually minimal. All other behavior of a tenured faculty

member, from advising degree candidates to preparing lectures to coming to the office in a bathing suit every day, is, for all intents and purposes, beyond review by the university. Tenure is a guarantee of lifetime employment. No matter how bad his teaching reviews come out, no matter how few grad students he graduates, and no matter how many temper tantrums he has with the support staff, the tenure holder cannot be fired.

The tenure process takes four or five years, during which time the tenure-seeker must grow an impressive portfolio of academic accomplishment and service to the university. He must sit on committees, show a constant flow of research funds, graduate a handful of Ph.D.'s, teach classes, and create his own classes that generate respectable enrollment. The tenure decision is made by a layer cake of committees: department, division, college, university, board of directors, all the way to the top. Some schools only really care about one or two aspects of performance, regardless of the smorgasbord of requirements to which they pay lip service. Smaller schools may heavily weight teaching quality, whereas many large research universities only count research dollars. If this assistant professor fails to achieve tenure, he is out of a job and must start the half-decade process all over again at another institution.

For the tenure seeker, the clock is ticking, and therefore so is yours. If he doesn't get tenure, you are out an advisor and degree as much as he is out of a job. While trying to satisfy the demanding requirements of a tenured portfolio, you may get muscled out for the sake of his career. He must publish or perish, and will frequently push for you to get journal articles out the door as quickly as possible. Needing to be first author for tenure, he may crowd you out to the end of the list of authors.

The tenure seeker needs grant money, and precious time not spent on research is spent on writing grants. He writes grant proposals non-stop while you do the research to support them. During crunch time, he makes you write grant proposals as well, albeit with his name on them. Don't expect to see this advisor in person too often. He's out and about networking, finding new sources of grant money, and paying court to people who already gave him money.

3. **The Checked-Out Tenure Holder.** This advisor is a tired and defeated specimen, content to spend his last professional decade or two in resplendent academic indolence. He acquired tenure some years back, and after an initial push of productivity, has lost the drive to carry on. Securing a job for life has seduced him into listlessness, and he has, to put it bluntly, checked out. He needn't work if he doesn't want to, and he has distinctly lost the drive that got him into his esteemed position. The checked-out tenure holder continues to take on students, as he enjoys standing atop the research-group hierarchy. Advising students makes him feel that he is still relevant, despite not having done research himself in years and having forgotten how to do much of it anyway. He does contribute to the field through his advising of grad students, but the contribution is vicarious. His network has withered over the years, and he eventually stops seeking funding entirely. Without any fresh contacts, he cannot gauge who has the money and what they want for it. Now he focuses only on the problems that interest him, and laments that no one will pay him for it like they used to.

4. **The Imminent Retiree.** This species of advisor has been around the block, published his papers, paid his dues, and is ready to enjoy the good life without those meddling grad students. The years have been good to the imminent retiree, but the time is rapidly approaching when he must pack it in and call it a life. He takes on progressively fewer grad students, looking to push them out quickly so he can move on (or lest he move on unexpectedly to a "better" place). Sometimes the imminent retiree holds on, fixating on one final goal, a last hurrah. It may be getting published in a particular journal, or solving one nagging 30-year-old problem. Regardless, everyone in the department knows he needs to go, but the power of tenure means he won't go away until he's good and ready.

There are two subsets of the imminent retiree. First, there is the napping octogenarian. This kind-hearted individual should have retired twenty years ago. He holds on for the sheer love of the work or the need to maintain some purpose in life. He almost certainly has no students. The octogenarian is frequently found at his desk napping (possibly expired, but no one is willing to check if he's still breathing). Despite these drawbacks, he possesses an extraordinary wealth of knowledge. Decades of experience give him incredible insight into his field, and you are well served to consult him as you proceed with your research. He also has an extraordinary wealth of chit-chatting skills, and you are advised to block off at least an hour for each visit to his office to account for inevitable talk about the weather and the project he worked on in 1962 that no one remembers.

The second subset is the sexist octogenarian, a sad figure who can't truly be held responsible for his behavior, being merely a product of his generation. This advisor comes from a time when women simply didn't do science or engineering. No matter how much times have changed, this member of the old guard can never be comfortable with ladies roaming about the lab (and probably showing too much ankle). He has a hard time concealing his contempt and condescension for female students, and needless to say he has none of his own. Unfortunately, the sexist octogenarian can still wield a great deal of influence in the department, on account of his age and professional position.

5. **The Slave Driver.** This character is prominent in the world of wet labs, where experiments are carried out in large numbers around the clock and demand constant human attention. At the risk of being politically incorrect, this type of advisor is especially common among faculty from foreign countries, which may have a different work ethic and where the competition to succeed may be much stiffer, requiring a slave-driving effort on their own part to reach their position today. Other types of advisors temporarily transform into the slave-driver under special circumstances, such as with an imminent tenure decision, but there are some who have always been and always will be in this mode.

The slave driver follows unconventional hours, coming into the office at noon and staying until midnight. He expects you to accommodate those hours and does not hesitate to schedule group meetings at 8 p.m. on Friday. The slave driver demands that you work at least as many hours as he, and preferably more. If you aren't in the lab 16 hours a day, then clearly you don't deserve to be in his research group. On the rare occasion that you impertinently request half a day off for life-saving surgery, you will be expected to make up the time on some other day. Much like the control freak, the slave driver monitors your progress at all times; unlike the control freak, however, he lets you work independently for the most part, as long as you never see the Sun or contemplate recreation of any kind.

6. **The AWOL.** This is the prominent and famous researcher whom everyone wants for an advisor. You've hit the jackpot. He will do wonders for your resume, but you will hardly ever see him in the many years of your grad school career. The absent-without-leave advisor made millions selling the rights to a few patents and has an entire library of books he's written. He is out of town, out of country, out of continent, almost at all times. He is in demand to speak at conferences, to give keynote lectures at universities, to sit on the boards of a dozen grant-giving agencies, and to advise a flock of young start-up companies flush with venture capital. In other words, he's too busy being an all-around famous person to deal with you. His research group is large enough to have developed its own hierarchy of post-docs, grad students, and undergrad interns: a little university within the university. The AWOL advisor won't remember your name for the first couple of years, and most of your interaction is through the post-docs to whom the AWOL has delegated nearly all of his authority. Despite the challenges of working in this anonymous environment, when you do begin your job search near graduation, one phone call from your advisor lines you up a dozen job interviews, no questions asked.

This tenured and respected faculty member is also a headhunting hazard. There is a risk that this advisor will be offered a better position at another university. This risk is especially high if the advisor is prominent in the community but works at a not-so-prominent institution. If he packs up and goes, his research goes with him. Would you be willing to follow? A master's degree can be wrapped up quickly, but if you don't want to move, you may have to start over with your Ph.D.

7. **The Diamond in the Rough.** Alas, like the finest gems, this advisor is the rarest of them all. The diamond in the rough is a well-known, well-respected, and well-funded professor who somehow still manages to put in time to be an advisor for his students. He is the man who has made it professionally but hasn't let it get to his head, and he doesn't overburden himself with travel for superficial appearances. A graduate program with this advisor is challenging, no doubt, but you find yourself mostly content with the experience. Inevitably, the diamond in the rough in your department is not in your field, so you can't work for him.

How to Vet a Candidate Advisor

When you arrive at graduate school, you are burdened with a flurry of paper. Forms of every kind must be filled out in triplicate to sate the hungry university bureaucracy. Eventually, you will be handed a form that needs to be signed by your advisor, whether it's for course registration or fellowship applications or teaching appointments or getting an office. You've arrived at the university only a few days ago, you know no one, have never taken a class there, and now you're expected to already have an advisor signing off on all of these documents. Universities often have no separate pipeline for new students without an advisor, and an enormous pressure develops to settle on an advisor as quickly as possible, if only to get this intimidating paperwork out of the way. Being without an advisor in graduate school is like being a man without a country. The wheels of bureaucracy grind to a halt from the blank signature lines. There are many ways to acquire an advisor, and the dizzying paperwork of the university drives some students into making a poor decision just to satisfy the bureaucrats.

There are many kinds of advisors out there, but how can you tell them apart for real? Are you courting a Yoda for an advisor, or Darth Vader? You may have a baseline compatibility with an advisor based on the field of study, but there is also an ephemeral aspect of chemistry between the two of you. Do you, for lack of a better word, jive? If you're planning on a Ph.D., can you see yourself working with (or, more accurately, *for*) this professor for the next five or six years? If you can develop a positive chemistry and rapport with a professor, then you're a long way towards finding yourself an advisor. Many a grad student has gone into a research group loathing the advisor for the sake of standing in the shadow of his fame, but choosing an advisor for the sake of bragging rights seldom yields a happy life.

You should find out, either from the professor himself or from his students, how long it typically takes for students in his group to graduate. For an M.S., 1–3 years is typical, with a coursework-only master's on the short end and a full-blown thesis on the long. If you're looking to get a master's as a working degree (that is, to secure a bump in the pay scale), you can worry less about making a major contribution to the field, and you probably won't publish anything. In that case, you don't want to be around forever. An advisor whose master's students alone take three or more years would not be for you. A Ph.D. typically takes 4–7 years after undergrad, or 2–4 years after the master's degree.

If a potential advisor's students are uniformly on the long end of the time spectrum, it is worth investigating why. The advisor may be exceptionally careful about allowing students to graduate. After all, the students reflect on the advisor's reputation as much as the advisor on the students'. He may not want to graduate anyone unless they live up to his high standards. The question is, how high are these standards, and are you willing to pay the tax of an extra couple of years living up to them? This advisor's research may also be in a heavily studied and competitive field, where years of effort are necessary to make a new contribution.

Another cause of uniformly long graduation times is group malaise. Given the descriptions of the "Types of Advisors," you can imagine that some of them do little to inspire their students. In a toxic social and research environment, grad students lose motivation, and progress ceases. Sometimes groups (both in academia and the real world) develop bad karma. Keep an eye out for this symptom of a dysfunctional group. However, be careful not to mistake grad-student exhaustion (which appears in every research group!) with malaise.

On the other end of the spectrum, some advisors push grad students out with high frequency. These advisors may have a "lower" threshold for graduation, which is not inherently a bad thing. In grad school as in life, one must not let the perfect be the enemy of the good. Many grad students linger for years beyond their expiration date for the sake of only marginal improvements in an otherwise solid body of work. Advisors who graduate students quickly often do not look for the high-gloss polish of some other advisors, although the contribution to the field and the legitimacy of the degree is not in question. It depends on what your personality can accept. If you are an unrepentant perfectionist, you may not jive with an advisor who isn't.

An excellent way to sift through potential advisors is to read their papers, websites, and media. Find the professor's journal articles, conferences papers, and other published material. Read some of the papers that look most interesting and skim the rest, but certainly read all of the article titles. What journals are the articles published in? Are they top journals? Publishing in lower-end journals could be a warning sign. One clever trick is to check if the journals he publishes in have page charges (more on those in Chapter 8). If he never publishes in the pricey journals, it could be a warning sign the group is short on funding.

You may also find that a particular advisor-candidate publishes in the same handful of journals all the time. Over the course of many years, some researchers fall into a rut and remain locked in a narrow corner of their already narrowly defined field, in which case there may be only one or two or three journals to publish in. This situation dramatically reduces the exposure of the professor's research to the community and can pigeonhole his students early in their careers.

When you visit the professor's website, you have the chance to see what he wants to present to the world about his research. The professor usually lists at least topics of interest, and cross-referencing that list with his publication record will tell you what he's most interested in right now. Many professors list research interests on their website that they haven't actually worked on in years. Depending on the circumstances, if an older topic interests you, you might be able to convince the advisor to pick it up again, funding notwithstanding. Sometimes topics are dropped simply because a student graduates and there's no one available or interested at the time to inherit the project. He may have been waiting for you all along!

By far the best way to vet a potential advisor is to talk to his students, who will be far more candid about their advisor and their research than any website can ever be. When you have the chance to meet these grad students, ask them as many questions as you can. Everyone expects you to ask about research, but there is much more useful information you must mine for, the sort that doesn't make it into the university brochure. Some wise questions include:

1. *How often do you interact with your advisor?* It is woefully common for grad students to seldom see their advisor, but interaction is what you need to grow into a successful professional. If you are dealing with an AWOL advisor or a checked-out tenure holder, you may meet your advisor only once a month, or less frequently if he spends half of the year on another continent being important. It is up to you to decide what is reasonable. If you want or need a lot of attention, an absent advisor may not be for you.

2. *How easily can you get in contact with your advisor?* Even if he's away at a conference or a gala benefit or a coronation, you might survive as long as he reads his email.

3. *How prompt is your advisor in returning important communications?* When course registrations need a signature, a paper is ready for journal submission, or graduation forms are due, you want your advisor to be responsive on important matters.

4. *How frequently does your advisor seek out research funding?* Funding is the life-blood of research in the modern university, and a steady flow means the difference between working in a research lab or working as a teaching assistant. The answer to this question can help you sniff out the checked-out tenure holders and similar characters who have given up looking for research money.

5. *How much funding does your advisor have, and how much is on the horizon?* Some advisors hesitate to tell potential new

grad students how dire a funding situation may be, but his current grad students are acutely aware of what's going on. An advisor may be willing to take you on because he has money now, but you should ask his students how long he realistically expects to have money. If a big grant that funds a dozen students runs out in a couple of years and there's no certainty of a follow-on grant, you may be in a precarious position two years hence.

6. *Where does your advisor get his money?* This is where your judgment comes in. The advisor and even his current students may be optimistic about funding, but you should also read between the lines for yourself. If you find out where this advisor's grant money comes from, think about the technical, political, and financial stability of that resource over the next several years. For example, NASA's Institute for Advanced Concepts used to provide research funding for pie-in-the-sky futuristic concepts, and many professors depended on that one agency for their research. When NASA abruptly shut that division down, all those professors and their grad students were in a lot of trouble. Another example: research into alternative energy, such as wind and solar power, has been on the rise for years and no doubt will continue for some time, but a professor studying windmill design will probably have more resources in Indiana than Manhattan. On the political side, the tide of research money for controversial subjects, such as stem-cell research, ebbs and flows with whoever is in the White House.

7. *How does your advisor moderate collaborations?* Note that this is not how *well* does he moderate them, but *in what manner* does he moderate them. This advisor may be very hands-off, letting you fend for yourself with other groups and universities, or he may be intimately involved in the communication among collaborating groups. Interactions in some collaborations are a game of telephone, where results pass from grad student to advisor to collaborating professor to collaborating grad student and back. When the lines of communication go haywire, you'll want an advisor who knows what's going on and can smooth out conflicts that are above a grad student's pay grade.

8. *How frequently does your advisor attend conferences?* Another way to differentiate between the checked-out tenure holder and the tenure-seeker or slave driver. The tenure holder usually gives up on attending conferences, or goes only to socialize. Conferences, which are covered in detail in Chapter 7, are the prime venue for maintaining a professional network. An advisor with lots of funding and seeking more will be frequently away at conferences, staying abreast of the latest developments in the field and cultivating professional relationships.

9. *Is your advisor away a lot? Where does he go?* The traveling advisor can be hard to get hold of, but if he is prompt with communications even when he's away, there may be no problem. Traveling is expensive; if an advisor can afford to travel hither and yon on grant money, he can usually fund plenty of grad students, too.

10. *Why did you choose this advisor over the others in the department? Or over others at other universities?* This question is valuable for any interview, including when you're looking for a real job after grad school. You'll be able to find out if people work with someone because of the research or because of the advisor.

11. *How long have you been in the group, and how far along are you?* This question is socially awkward for grad students, since we don't like to talk about how little progress we feel we've made, but it's something you need to know. Some students are burdened with years and years of research and have hardly anything to show for it. Sometimes it's the fault of the student, sometimes the professor. You don't want to know "how far along" they are in terms of their research, which is too subjective to evaluate for you being a new or prospective grad student. Rather, you want to know how far along they are in the steps of the graduate program, especially for the Ph.D., which has several steps. When you know how many years they are into the program, find out if they have taken their qualifying exams yet (step 1 of the Ph.D.), or if they've done their research proposal (step 2).

Find out how far they think they are from graduation, if they dare to make a prediction.

12. *How frequently do you discuss the progress of your M.S. or Ph.D. program with your advisor?* You will certainly discuss your research with your advisor, at the very least because he's paying for it and wants to know how you are spending his valuable resources. However, you should also be talking about your personal progress in the program. You should find out if this potential advisor's students talk about their progress and about their future plans, or if they're on their own. This question helps to differentiate the true advisors (professors who want to guide and mold new professionals) from the pure researchers (who only care about their research and churn out grad students like widgets).

Looking up former students gives you an idea of how a candidate advisor's graduates fare in the real world. The professor's website may list former students, old journal articles have them listed as authors, and his current, senior grad students will know many of them. You can use the Internet to track some of them down and see where they are professionally today. Where do this advisor's students end up? They may be in industry, government, or academia. One of those sectors may dominate for his graduates, possibly because of the advisor's personal contacts, and you should consider if that is where you might like to go. An advisor with lots of friends in government agencies may have a harder time helping you find employment in industry.

How to Get an Advisor

For the lucky among you, you already know whom you want to work with. After reading up on many universities during the application process and selecting one, you go straight to the professor who interests you most. Wanting to work with one particular person saves time and grief at the start of grad school, but it also brings risks. Meeting with this potential advisor is like a job interview. If this professor doesn't take you on as his student, you're out of luck and might need to leave the school all together. Ideally, you will have spoken to him much earlier, such as during the prospective-student visit some weeks or months before, and gauged his interest in you. If you're going into a particular department blind (that is, they didn't pay for you to visit and you haven't met anyone), making your choice of school based on one professor is like playing the lottery. If you get in, you're golden, but if you don't, you may be unhappy with all of the other choices.

The luckiest among you already have an advisor when you get to grad school. This scenario is common for large, well-funded research groups, where the professor announces available positions similar to job postings. While you are still in undergrad, you should keep an eye out for these announcements, usually posted on the professors' or departments' websites. Contacting them ahead of time along with your application can put you on their radar, and any professors you're friendly with as an undergrad can help with this process. Word of mouth is king for graduate positions like these. If you catch the attention of someone at the grad school, you're flown in during the open house to meet as a grad student candidate with the professor, and he may tell you outright if you've got the position. Arriving at grad school in this case is a lot like starting a new job, and you are fortunate to bypass the anxiety of your fellow grad students as they seek advisors on their own.

A common way to find an advisor, especially in lab sciences, is through a rotation program administered by the department. Even grad students who already have an advisor coming in may be required to go through the program and get to know the breadth of research in the department. Rotations send you to three or four labs for a few months each, give you a taste of the research in that lab, and introduce you to the people working there. Although you may think you enjoy the research of a particular lab, working in that environment for a few months gives you the opportunity to learn if you jive with future coworkers and with the advisor himself. As with any other job, if you can't stand the people you spend your days with, you will be miserable.

A rotation program also helps the lab and professor evaluate you. The professor and other grad students are looking to see if you are competent. Many hopeless individuals slip through the cracks of the application process, and the lab needs to know that you won't unnecessarily slow them down. Inexperience, however, is not something to worry about. They know you are inexperienced. They want to see if you can learn. Someone inexperienced but competent can pick up rules, methods, and protocols quickly and work on their own in short order, saving the lab time and money. An incompetent individual, no matter how experienced they are, drags the whole operation down.

The professor also gauges your potential commitment to the lab if you choose them. Does it seem that you will actually be devoted—within reason—to the lab and your research? Many people float through grad school from lab to lab, refusing to commit to one group or project. These people frequently never finish grad school. Others announce publicly that they have other plans for their future and that grad school is a temporary detour. For example, an individual may enter grad school as a "break" from undergrad before applying to medical school. Although medical school is a noble goal, telling your future advisor that you might drop everything after a couple of years to do something else is no way to build a professional relationship. You should keep plans like these to yourself.

The most unpleasant, but sadly most common, method of getting an advisor is the free-for-all. At the start of the school year, packs of new grad students cluster around the offices of tenured faculty, each eagerly awaiting his or her turn to make an impression and, with any luck, land a coveted spot in some—in *any*—research group. I myself had to ambush my future advisor on more than one occasion, waiting to pounce at those precise moments before he had a class to teach, when his mind was elsewhere and more likely to sign the form I stuffed in his hand.

Without a walk-in guarantee ahead of time from an established research group, you have no choice but to hunt down the handful of professors whose work interested you during the school search. Some departments leave you on your own during this quest. During the free-for-all, you compete with the other grad students for an advisor, and while the number of professors is finite, the number of grad students is seemingly infinite. Another eager beaver is always waiting in the wings, looking to grab the professor's attention. This situation is particularly bad if a few professors have made names for themselves in a small department, and there's nowhere for the surplus to go. Professors do their best to avoid the hordes of new grad students looking for someone to sign their paperwork. Being an advisor is a major commitment for a faculty member, and there are only so many people one can handle.

The best way, bar none, to get an advisor is to talk to him. As early as you can, set up a meeting with a potential advisor. Each professor is inundated with emails from prospective students, and the medium is too impersonal to spark the student-advisor relationship. As mentioned in a previous chapter, bucking the email trend and calling a potential advisor on the telephone is a sure-fire way to get noticed. You can be sure that no one else will call, which sets you apart, and unlike an email, the professor has no choice but to engage in the conversation.

When you do manage to arrange a face-to-face meeting, you should facilitate as much give-and-take as possible. You should chat about yourself and your research interests, but you should be sure to ask the professor about their work. Usually they'll talk your ear off about their past and current research. You have to make sure that this is something that interests you. If you haven't been able to go on rotations in different labs, this meeting is important to get a feel for whether you see yourself studying this topic for years.

Getting into the professor's research group should be a topic of conversation at this meeting. Many meek students wait for the professor to bring it up himself, or drop hints here and there about research interests. Fortune favors the bold! Ask outright what their availabilities, expectations, and requirements are for getting into the group. Many professors will have an answer for you then and there. Some have metrics they use to gauge your suitability to do research with them. They may identify a critical stage at which a decision is made about admitting you to the group: it may be completing certain classes, spending some time in the lab as an underling, or performing some extra introductory research task.

Above all, make sure that a potential advisor knows who you are. Many people parade past a professor's desk at the start of a semester, and it's easy for everyone to muddle together. You must stand out and be noticed. Talk to them directly. Take their classes. Get high grades in their classes, show an interest in their research, and demonstrate a basic competence. (Do not, however, exert effort to impress them. The teacher's pet alienates both the professor, who is looking for a future peer and not a servant, and your classmates, who are now actually your colleagues. You will be surprised how many grad students—people now mostly in their mid-twenties!—revert to this grade-school behavior.)

Dealing with Your Advisor

Your advisor is a lot like a CEO, and your relationship with him is very different from that with your fellow grad students or with professors when you were an undergraduate. Usually he's not even doing research himself. He's certainly not doing *your* research. Rather, he's *managing* research, which is a completely different responsibility. He has to keep track of deadlines for multiple projects simultaneously while herding a flock of grad students, placating collaborators, and wooing funding agencies. Your advisor must cope with finding new grad students to replace the graduating ones, and he must constantly seek out new research money to fund them. The eternal quest for grant money is time consuming and requires a lot of travel and networking. You can imagine, then, that your relationship is not the same as when you took Physics 101 from this professor four or five years ago.

When beginning your life in grad school, you must keep in mind that your advisor doesn't know the answers. That's why they call it "research." Otherwise it would just be more "school." He can provide guidance and assistance, but in many ways you're on your own. A good advisor steers you away from fruitless avenues of research and points you in the right direction for surmounting your latest hurdle, but you have to tackle the big challenges yourself. You have to teach yourself the academic material that you missed in undergrad, and you have to learn how to function in a real lab on your own. Your advisor won't do this for you.

Approaching your advisor for "advising" is a delicate matter. You must use your advisor like a tool. He serves a particular purpose, and he is not a panacea, no more than you would use a hammer to screw in a nail. When trouble strikes in your research, the knee-jerk reaction is to run to your advisor, but you need to know, first of all, if it really is trouble. Try to solve this problem yourself first. Think of all the ways that you could get around or solve this problem, and keep track of how each possible solution failed or affected the output. Consult other people in the research group. It's possible someone else has run into the problem before.

When you're out of all other possibilities, you have leave to trouble your advisor. You should be as specific as possible. A comment like "I don't know why this doesn't work" is not helpful. "I don't know what this variable means" is better, but "should I use chemical X or chemical Y in this assay?" is best. Have a specific question ready for your advisor when you go into his office, and know what you want to get out of the meeting. Do you need a specific course of action, or broader guidance? You must be prepared to describe all of the things that you already tried to solve the problem: one of the first things your advisor will ask is, "What have you already tried?" If you're lucky, your advisor will have a good idea, but there is of course the chance that he will be as stumped as you.

One subtle detail lost on many new grad students is that your advisor is not a member of the university bureaucracy. The professors do not interact with the school in the same way as students. They are employees, and their professional day-to-day life rarely intersects with the paperwork demands made on students. Each school imposes many rules and regulations regarding the completion of your degree, and your advisor doesn't know them. You should not bother your advisor with questions about bureaucratic process, like credit-hour requirements, forms, course prerequisites, and so on. You should direct those questions to the staff. The rules have no doubt changed many times since he's been at the institution, and I wouldn't trust the accuracy of what my advisor thinks the answer is.

You should also know your advisor's limits. Don't bother him with something he has no chance of helping with. If your advisor still uses an Apple II in his office and only uses it to check email, it is a waste of time to ask him about how to implement a new algorithm. You also can't expect him to offer exceptionally time-consuming help, like debugging your computer code. He doesn't have the time or the intimate knowledge of your work to be useful. Keep your interactions with your advisor to the areas where you know he can help.

The relationship with your advisor is first and foremost a professional one. You should respect your advisor, but do not worship him. Even the most famous people are human. Your famous advisor has faults and vices. He farts and burps and argues with his teenage children. If you build an aura in your head around this man, you are guaranteed to be disappointed, and you don't want resentment to define the majority of your years with this advisor.

You must respect yourself, as well. You've studied long and hard to get where you are, and you know what you know, so stand by it. As you progress in your program, your advisor increasingly becomes a peer rather than a superior. You must be willing to speak up. Stand your ground when you are justified, and gracefully acknowledge when you are wrong. *Acting* like a peer, rather than a cowering underling, is what *makes* you a peer. A firm but respectful attitude to your advisor reciprocates respect back to you. If a professor refuses to return the respect you offer him and instead demands fearful servants for grad students, then that advisor is not for you.

Chapter 4

The Research Group

The primary organization for research is the "group," all the members of which have the same advisor, who is often referred to as the "PI" (Principal Investigator). Each member of a group is funded by your advisor's research grants, or your advisor is at least responsible—in theory—for finding ways to fund all of his students, perhaps as teaching assistants. Within a research group, members are often assigned to work together on projects, but each member must simultaneously have his or her own responsibilities and goals. Each person needs their own, original work to graduate.

The research group is a small corporation. The PI is the CEO, the manager, who is responsible for bringing in revenue, better known as grant money. After the group pays taxes to the university for facilities and overhead, the employees (the grad students) get paid. This pseudo-corporation's product is journal articles and technical reports, which the funding agencies pay dearly for. Government research agencies fund journal articles for the sake of science; real-world corporations fund articles and reports to support their business, and a particularly productive research group may also file patents on new inventions and copyrights on important documentation. Your group may even have a special name, usually an acronym, with a trademarked logo. This branding makes the research group all but identical to a small business, except that it is not obligated to pay its grad-student employees a living wage or benefits. In return, the grad students go about their work hoping one day to acquire a degree of their own that will let them, in turn, create their own mini-corporation at another institution, and thus the cycle continues.

The research group provides a sounding board for each member's work. When you start doing research, and even as the years go by, you have times when you can't progress any further, when you're spinning your wheels. The other members of the group are there to offer advice and to support you. They cannot do your research for you, but the group is there so that you aren't alone in the wilderness. Your advisor won't be there all the time. In fact, he may not be there very often at all. Your fellow group members are with you in the trenches, in the same lab. They deal with the same equipment, the same support staff, the same professors, and the same classes, and in many aspects of your research they are in a far better position than your advisor to help. Your advisor sets the strategy of the research, but the research group works together and executes the tactics to get results.

Research groups, like universities, are entrenched in medieval tradition, and most follow rigid hierarchies following the general scheme in Figure 1.

The PI sits atop the totem pole; your advisor, the professor, determines where everyone else lives in the hierarchy, both via his authority to permit your passage through the milestones of grad school and by social favoritism. More than a few grad students have reached the top "before their time" by virtue of indulging and manipulating their advisor's personality in all the right ways.

Immediately below the PI are the post-docs, who have finished their Ph.D.'s and are learning how to become professors themselves. The PI delegates most quotidian research-group responsibilities to the post docs: they monitor the progress of the other grad students and the status of research grants, coordinate publications, and prepare new research proposals for the PI.

The senior grad students—the Ph.D. candidates—toil below the post docs in eager anticipation of doctoral glory. Further below them are the junior grad students, the Ph.D. students (who haven't yet passed an examination of their research proposal) and the M.S. students. The lowest members of the research-group hierarchy are the undergrads. Undergraduates are not members of the group in the strictest sense—they aren't working on their own research program and haven't been admitted to the gradu-

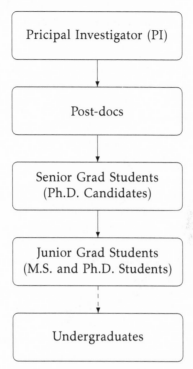

Figure 1: The Research Group Hierarchy

ate school—but you are bound to have a handful of them scurrying about the lab, assigned the most tedious and trivial tasks and causing trouble all the way.

As in any bureaucracy, *longevity* determines your height in the research group's social ladder, not talent. Your accomplishments relative to your peers are irrelevant in this ranking. A conference or journal article may spread your fame far and wide, but in the research group, your starting year determines your status. Also as in every bureaucracy, those at the top guard their privileges with a jealousy inversely proportional to their value. (Why are faculty rivalries so vicious? Because the stakes are so small!) Ironically, being at the top of the research group has no real perks associated with it. Older students can sometimes coerce younger group members to perform unpleasant or tedious tasks in lab, but otherwise, seniority in the research group is merely a reminder of how long you've been languishing in your graduate program!

The size of your research group is a major factor in the lab's culture, but there are no distinct lines between large and small groups. As you get to know your own group and see how the members of other groups interact, you will find that each group has its own attitude, its own mojo.

Large groups have 15–30 members, or more. Famous AWOL advisors with fountains of research funding may operate several labs at the same time, all working on different projects, and those labs demand substantial manpower to operate. These large groups are miniature kingdoms all on their own. The PI is the feudal lord, but he is away from the castle so often that he delegates his authority to the most senior squires, the post-docs. The post-docs are the lieutenants, who oversee a project as a whole and have the authority to direct you, the underling grad student, to perform whatever experiments they deem necessary. From the post-docs on down, the seniority descends year by year: the Ph.D. candidates, the Ph.D. students, the second- and first-year grad students, and the lowliest peasants, those undergrad interns.

In a gargantuan research group, the PI may not know everybody. He may not remember your name for the first year, unless you make an effort to get noticed. Working in a large group means less personal contact with your advisor, and interaction with a "higher authority" on your research may come through the post-docs instead. With multiple students working together on large projects, the lines blur between where one student's work ends and yours begins, making it harder to develop a research plan for graduation. These close quarters can also lead to competition within the group, both for funding and for attention. However, large groups are large because there's lots of research funding, and joining a large group may involve trading individual attention for the security of guaranteed funding. A large group is also led by a well-known advisor, which can help your resume and your career in the long run.

Small research groups have fewer than 10 members and resemble a family more than a fiefdom. You have plenty of one-on-one contact with your advisor, and he is able to take more interest in your personal progress. Fewer students in the group means less competition, making it easy to carve out your own corner of a project for your research plan, and it is possible to make a research project entirely your own. There may be no post-docs at all in a small research group, which leaves you responsible for taking part in the high-level goings on, such as grant-writing and communicating with your advisor's colleagues. Being a big fish in this small pond offers you more exposure for the same amount of effort as in a larger group.

Being in a small group also means that you often work alone. You may find solitude desirable, but the isolation prevents anyone else in the group, including your advisor, from following the details of your work. You may have no one to approach when small problems crop up, and seeking help from a fellow group member may demand extensive explanations before you even ask your question. The risk of spinning your wheels and getting nowhere is higher in a small group, and if you make a mistake somewhere along the line, no one may catch it. In fact, if you produce good results on a regular basis, you receive less pushback over time to justify them, and errors can creep in without noticing. Life in any group requires constant vigilance and returning to first principles to ensure the validity of your results, as you may be the only one who can.

Group Meetings

The lifeblood of a successful research group, large or small, is communication. Quality work flourishes only when grad students, post docs, and professors talk openly, freely, and often about their work and their progress. Aside from the griping among fellow grad students in off-campus bars—where all the really inspired ideas come from—most communication in a research group occurs in group meetings. Not all research groups have regularly scheduled meetings, but most do. The frequency of the meetings depends on your advisor, with weekly or biweekly meetings most common.

Every group meeting involves presenting your most recent research results, typically in a PowerPoint presentation-style format. These meetings above all keep your advisor informed of progress in your research and in your academic plans. Your advisor and fellow group members can offer critical review of your work, and you have the opportunity to point out problem areas where you need help.

Communication is a two-way street, which means you need to contribute in group meetings yourself. These meetings far too often involve a silent audience of grad students waiting for the advisor to say something to a trembling presenter. You must speak up and provide the critical commentary that you yourself need when you are that trembling presenter on stage. Offering one helpful comment gets the ball rolling; starting a conversation about the presentation breaks the tension and triggers the collaborative energy that research is all about. If your years in grad school involve working alone in your cubicle, interrupted only by infrequent presentations to people who have nothing to say, your experience will be unpleasant and long.

Getting Along with Other Groups

In an era where buzzwords like "interdisciplinary," "synergistic," and "teamwork" guarantee all the funding in the world, collaboration with another research group is undeniably in your future. No single group is enough to get funding for a full-scale project these days, and navigating the waters of collaboration is another skill you need as a grad student, especially for those sticky situations when your advisor isn't around to calm the storm.

Collaboration among research groups is *supposed* to bring together the strengths of its constituent parts to achieve a common goal. In reality, it crams together conflicting agendas and inflated egos, interested more in the fair distribution of grant funding than the efficient execution of experiments, which are performed by grad students who have little to gain by sharing credit for their work.

At the head of a project is the PI, the primary investigator, a "first among equals" with the co-PIs, who run the collaborating research groups. The lead PI is the voice of the research project to the outside world, communicating with the funding agency and ensuring that the project remains on schedule. From a research perspective, the leadership may not be as cut and dry, and it ebbs and flows over the course of a project. Each group contributes a unique set of talents to achieve the project's goals. At the beginning of a project one group may be instrumental, whereas later the influence shifts to another group with a different set of skills.

Funding in a collaborative project is divided among the participating groups. The PIs determine well in advance how that money is divided, and the funding level is determined primarily by labor cost (that is, grad-student work time) and consumable costs (e.g., lab materials). If group A needs one semester's worth of funding and group B needs two, group B gets budgeted for twice as much money, no matter that group A may contribute 75% of the final content. This distribution tends to promote lethargic research speeds, because professors have a vested interest in taking as long as possible to maximize their slice of the pie.

When funding isn't as plentiful as you would like, you may end up participating in the inter-group black market. If you want to graduate, the work needs to get done, and to get it done you may need resources your group doesn't have. Even if you're not part of an official collaboration, unofficial ones spring up by virtue of having something everyone else needs. Mobile resources, like lab equipment, are often lent and borrowed. The terms of such loans are ambiguous and the costs, if any, are unspecified, but the etiquette of a real collaboration applies. You may owe the other group a favor down the road, or you may end up bartering a piece of equipment of your own. It is important not to presume that you can use someone else's equipment because you work in the same physical space. When ownership of a resource is clearly defined (and the owner isn't you), you are obligated to get permission first. Otherwise you have no idea whose work you delay or damage.

Communication is the bedrock of a successful collaboration, but it may seem like groups speak completely different languages. As in any relationship, tensions due to poor communication are bound to grow. For example, consider three researchers sitting in a room: a mathematician, a biologist, and a physicist, and all three are collaborating on a grant to study the spread of an epidemic in a city. The physicist is worried about developing a tractable model and wants to assume infected patients are point masses, the quarantined city is a perfect gas, and the virus propagates through perfectly inelastic collisions with healthy people. The biologist is concerned instead about identifying the vectors for infection, determining the rate of replication, and measuring fatality rates. Meanwhile, the mathematician wants to solve a lemma to the Lotka-Volterra equations. Who's right here? Is anybody? All three want to solve the same problem, but they approach it in very different ways. The challenge of collaboration is to get all three of these people talking the same language—however briefly—so that they can align priorities and develop a plan of action for their research. Large projects pull in talent from many fields. Not everyone talks about problems in the same way, and not everyone *thinks* about problems in the same way. Even a choice of variable names can spark conflict.

Many projects are linear (that is, each task follows another in sequence), and waiting for results can be a source of frustration and conflict. When you are handed a project, and another group depends on your results before they can do anything, you should learn what is expected of you and when. You should be professional and not make the other groups wait unreasonably long, but only your collaborators and your advisor can tell you what unreasonable is. If you're working on a problem that takes longer than expected, you should let the follow-on groups know about the delay as soon as possible. If frustrated grad students are banging on your door looking for results, you've waited too long to communicate.

Sometimes groups agree to collaborations that are beyond their abilities. When the promise of research funding beckons, some researchers over-extend themselves and cannot produce what their PIs promised. This behavior is not inherently duplicitous. It is hard to say no to a funding opportunity, and rather than admitting that they can't do the work, these groups delay results or revise the results that they do distribute when they find inevitable errors. If you're a victim of this situation, you'll have to find a way around it. You can speak to your advisor, but complaining won't get you what you need. Your advisor can't influence much, especially once a collaboration is under way. Rather, you have to hope that you can make some use of the results you do get, or, if worse comes to worse, do some of the work yourself.

Under the radar of the advisors and PIs, personal conflicts can develop among grad students in different groups. Sometimes cultural differences interfere with a harmonious collaboration. Researchers may have different notions about punctuality and different interpretations of personal property and politeness. Many cultures have different expectations about interaction with the sexes that can come as quite a surprise. I have known female grad students who conflicted with foreign male counterparts over who was responsible for doing grunt work or even who should speak first in research meetings. These issues are known to exist, and you are bound to encounter them at some point. How you deal with these conflicts determines your happiness in the long run. Venting to your advisor, if he is the indulgent type, is a way to get some frustration off your chest. These days it would be considered impolite to confront someone for this "culture-conflict" behavior, but it also too much trouble (and with events often undocumented) to lodge a formal complaint. Grad school is a small taste of the cultural misunderstandings you will encounter in the real world, where you are expected to tolerate even the most ridiculous behavior, especially if it's from a paying customer. You should get used to it now. Stay professional, grit your teeth, and try to minimize your interaction with individuals you conflict with.

Group Rivalries

The flip side to collaboration is rivalry. When research areas overlap and skills are duplicated, collaboration is no longer possible. Instead, you compete for resources that both groups are able to use effectively, and, alas, there are only so many resources to go around. Collaborations may be impossible because of personality differences (some professors just don't get along), there may be insurmountable geographic differences (groups in New Zealand and Chicago can't share the same lab), or, simply, "this town ain't big enough for the two of us." Some scientific results just don't need the collaboration that other projects do. Everyone talks a good game when it comes to collaboration, but everyone also wants all the credit they can get. If two groups have the same skills, there's nothing to gain by diluting journal articles with extra co-author collaborators whom you don't need in the first place.

At this breaking point, you end up with two groups fighting for attention and publications in the same field on the same topic. Competition is good in theory—it encourages efficiency in your research, because you don't want to get scooped—but it also introduces stress into your life. Some groups compete at the same university or in the same department. When two professors have a falling out, they retreat to their respective offices and can divert an astonishing amount of energy and malice to upstaging their competitor, both in the professional world and on faculty committees. These intra-departmental rivalries are poisonous, and they are not uncommon. One university in the United States, which shall remain anonymous, has an engineering department with notoriously dysfunctional faculty relations, where two battling camps operate each from their own building and regularly strive to sink the tenure hopes of young faculty in the opposing cabal. Another department across the country is known for shouting matches during faculty meetings, and this noxious atmosphere has driven away many talented faculty applicants.

Some group rivalries are actually professor rivalries that spill over to the grad students. In this situation, an inter-group underground may develop. Namely, the grad students maintain civil relationships, but keep them a secret so as not to raise the ire of their advisors. When two such "competing" groups have complementing skills the grad students need, collaboration does happen, even if the advisors don't want it. After a friend of mine raised a ruckus by asking for help from a student in another group with a hostile advisor, the two students went underground. Meetings between grad students in the groups were planned in secret, and they met off campus to reduce the risk of being discovered.

These professorial personality wars are a product of the environment that professors live in, where they are seldom brought to task for their egos or behavior. What starts as a differing view on methodology turns into a battle over equipment purchases and space usage, which turns into a war over admissions policies and faculty hiring. More than one department out there is known to divide into camps between powerful and well-funded faculty. These faculty members fight over money, secretaries, facilities, committees, tenure, and coffee flavors in the break room. Under the best of circumstances, they simply avoid all interaction. As their worst, grad students are used as pawns in ongoing battles where no one can win. The best thing a grad student can do is to avoid these groups, and if you're lucky, the battles will rage behind closed doors at faculty meetings.

Getting Scooped

You're sitting in your office in the early morning, sipping your coffee, and you pull out the latest issue of your favorite journal. You skim the table of contents. An article title—eerily similar to the one you're working on—catches your eye, and your heart stops. That's definitely not your name in the list of authors. You frantically turn to the offending pages and read the abstract: the same hypothesis, the same experiments, even the same conclusions that you yourself have neatly recorded in the research notebook on your desk, waiting for you to get around to typing them up. The grad student's worst nightmare has just happened to you: you've been scooped!

When rivalries stretch across academic borders, the battlefield ends up in scholarly journals and conferences. It's hard to know what your competitors are doing until they do it. New papers are published without warning, and there is a risk that your research will be scooped. The race to publish becomes all-consuming, leading to long nights as you prepare journal submissions as quickly as you can. The race to patent may be even more exhausting. Patents are where the big money is made, and you must be first with a patent application. Patents are the most damning place to be scooped: published papers are refereed by peers, but patents are refereed by federal law.

Scooping is the worst part of a rivalry, because it directly affects you and your graduation. Watching the pertinent journals helps you keep an eye on the doings of other research groups. You never want to be scooped on your hard-earned results. It happens sometimes, but there are several ways around it without having to throw away all of your work, which is what you'll feel like doing the first time it happens to you.

The most popular maneuver around scooped research is to redefine your goals. Your methods and results will differ in some ways from the scooping article, and you can pretend that you were planning to do something else all along. If you reassess the interpretation of your own results, you may find that you have something completely different to say than the other group.

Alternatively, you can publish scooped results anyway, confirming the other group's work. The essence of research and science is reproducibility, after all. As long as you can provide a unique-enough take on your work to get past the reviewers, it doesn't make a difference if you got scooped. You may not make a splash, but you might still get published, which brings you one step closer to graduation.

Lastly, you may be able to build off of the scooped research immediately. After you've spent months preparing your experiments, all of the apparatus is still in place to continue. You no doubt still have lingering research questions, and the competing group will have discussed its own planned follow-on work. You may have already done more than the competing group in another area of the project, and if you work quickly enough, you could scoop the scoopers!

Chapter 5

Your Research

In grad school, a new stage of your intellectual evolution begins. After years of cracking the books, it's time to open the door to a lab and start practicing everything your professors have preached. Performing research is your chance to contribute to a community and to a body of knowledge that has been growing for a thousand years. Your part may be large or small, but you are going to have a part.

By the time you are done with grad school, you will be an expert in an exquisitely isolated and obscure subject. You can revel in the knowledge that for a brief time you know everything there is to know about something; that no one anywhere in the world and no one who has ever lived has known as much about this tiny corner of the cosmos as you. When you reached that limit of human knowledge, you pushed it back a little bit.

Every now and then one must step away from the cynicism engendered by life in grad school. Sentimentalism about "expanding the frontiers of knowledge" may be overwrought, but even a cold and heartless pragmatist must enjoy the recognition that, in research, you are jealously pursuing a small slice of immortality.

The Myth of the Scientific Method

So what is research, anyway? Everyone remembers what elementary school taught us about how science works: you formulate a question, compose a hypothesis that may answer your question, run an experiment to test the hypothesis, then see if the experiment confirms your hypothesis. Repeated confirmation of your hypothesis through experimentation elevates it to a "theory" (and, after even more confirmation, to a "law"). This whole process is supposed to be "research." Poll the average citizen, and most of them assume that researchers formulate questions over breakfast, concoct hypotheses in the morning, break for lunch, do experiments in the afternoon, and check the results over dinner, rinse and repeat. Science!

This method is reasonable and comprehensible, and what a shame that practical research seldom resembles it at all. In practice, research is any investigation that you can publish or—even better—that someone will pay you for. As you contemplate your own research and formulate a plan with your advisor, you may be shocked to find that you never clearly define a hypothesis of any kind. For all the talk about writing a Ph.D. "thesis," many theses have no thesis at all. Science has become so diversified that hypothesis makers and experimentalists are often different people with different research programs and priorities: planetary scientists make hypotheses about the formation of solar systems, but it's a different set of scientists who power up their telescopes and actually look for these solar systems.

These planet-hunting astronomers are part of a major component of scientific activity: data gathering. Cataloguing has been a noble scientific pursuit for hundreds of years. In the seventeenth and eighteenth centuries, Europeans spread out across the globe documenting every fern and nematode they found, dropping a few in formaldehyde, and moving on to the next island. To this day, many researchers and grad students make substantial contributions just by finding new stuff: astronomers discover new planets, biologists discover new species of frogs, archaeologists uncover families of dinosaur fossils. Still other researchers make a living and contribution by monitoring and characterizing known objects: observing the changes in Jupiter's atmosphere, taking a census of endangered species, tracking the migration of humpback whales. These researchers without a doubt contribute to their field, but they are a cog in the machine of the scientific method.

In fact, serendipity is probably the strongest influence in research, especially the most influential research. Many grad students toil in their offices trying to prove a theorem or develop a better toaster, but the most groundbreaking contributions to science and engineering tend to happen by accident. A fortuitous observation in a lab leads a researcher down a train of thought that he or she never would have imagined, and shortly thereafter they're publishing a paper in *Nature*.

If you scroll through the list of Nobel laureates every year, most of them receive their award "for the discovery of..." They owe their Nobel to being in the right place at the right time, and having the wherewithal to capitalize on an opportunity when it was presented to them. Did these researchers work incredibly hard? Of course. Did they work harder than their colleagues down the hall? Nope.

But serendipity is not the exclusive domain of famous scientists. Any grad student can benefit by exploiting random chance to get one step closer to graduation. My first publication was the result of a complete accident. After weeks of tedious numerical modeling my research was going nowhere. It was late. I was hungry and tired. In a moment of frustration I switched a number in an equation from 1 to 2, hoping to choke the computer code as punishment for its intransigence, and ran it...and out came a stable simulation far better than anything I had hoped to find. I spent the next week playing with my new discovery, impressed my advisor, and had a conference paper ready to go in a month. The only trick to enjoying serendipity: I couldn't let anyone know. My paper had to make it seem like I had planned to change that equation all along.

The scientific method tells you to perform an experiment to test your hypothesis, but it's not so easy to design and execute an experiment. For many researchers, experimentation is completely infeasible, either due to resources, consequences of failure, or time. Astronomers hypothesize about Neptune's atmosphere, but a space mission to Neptune costs billions of dollars that nobody is willing to pay. Research into experimental drugs is hampered by the consequences of failure: dead human subjects. And climate scientists hypothesize about the state of the Earth's atmosphere in thousands of years, but there is no time to see if they're right.

But if you can do experiments, the biggest challenge you will have in research is reconciling the messy results of your experi-

ments with your original problem statement. Once you've run a
month's worth of experiments, you have megabytes of data to sort
through. Is that outlier a bad data point, or is it just "ugly"? Is
it an inevitable statistical fluctuation, or did something actually
go wrong? Can you make a credible argument to remove it? Will
your conclusions change if you do remove it?

And as you dig deeper into your data, statistics rears its ugly
head. Many fields rely heavily on statistics to glean conclusions
from their data, particularly fields—like economics, psychology,
medicine, and biology—that deal with people and living things,
which are hard to quantify with theories and laws. Human systems are unpredictable, there are hundreds of variables, and it
may be impossible to define a control. Statistics is a valuable tool
to sift through the chaos. For many M.S. and Ph.D. programs,
only a third of your time is spent doing actual experiments; the
rest goes into running statistics on your data, massaging the numbers, and tweaking the p-values, so that with any luck you might
have something meaningful to say and creep closer to graduation.

Cataloguing, monitoring, serendipity, and statistics. This is
much of the research you will see and do in grad school. Any single individual's interaction with (or career in) research will seldom resemble the scientific method from start to finish—except,
perhaps, in broad strokes drawn at the conclusion of a journal article.

We're Not in Undergrad Any More

Undergrad was carefully crafted theater, where every question has
its answer, and every answer is unquestionable. Your professor always has those answers tucked away, ready to wield them when
hapless students come calling at office hours. Examples in class
apply simplifying assumptions to illustrate concepts, and take advantage of hopelessly unrealistic models. As a physics student, I
saw humans modeled as perfect spheres to calculate their electrical capacitance, atoms modeled as miniature solar systems, and
ham modeled as a perfect gas to demonstrate diffusion of heat
through a medium. Simplifications like these occur throughout
your undergraduate experience in science or engineering.

The real world of research is far less convenient. All of the easy problems have already been solved, and simplifying assumptions may be harder to come by. In fact, it can be exceptionally difficult just to formulate and express a new problem, much less solve it. You are expected to describe the question your research asks and what precisely your "thesis" is. These are two very tough questions to pose, before you even start trying to research answers to them. The road to completing research, if it can be completed at all, is never straight. Real research if filled with uncertainty, roadblock after roadblock, and occasional serendipity. It's only after the answers are in hand that we go back and make it look like we knew what we were doing all along.

As you begin research, the community will reveal to you a new level of sophistication in thought and method that you have never encountered before. Rising up through the ranks in undergrad is regular and linear. There is a set time at which you complete each rank (i.e., a semester), and the problems and classes become progressively harder on a predictable scale. In grad school, you are immediately dumped from those last, coddling senior-year classes into the professional academic world. This world is not just "another step" above senior-level courses. It's an immediate jump from the kiddie pool to the deep end. Professionals always work at the cutting edge. It is the only way to compete. They work on the hardest problems (because that's usually all that's left!), bringing to bear all of the techniques and methods that exist. Even in technical areas that you studied intensively in undergrad and that you felt you knew fairly well, the current research and journal articles will look alien and far advanced of anything you learned thus far. You're now working with people who've been doing this research for 40 years, and you have to catch up in a flash.

You have no choice but to adapt to this new environment. It may seem like everyone around you knows everything that's going on and you don't, but don't let this perception overwhelm you. Sometimes it's beneficial to have a reality check that you're not as smart as you thought you were, especially after sailing through those last classes in undergrad. As you start reading papers and progressing in your research, you'll pull out a lot of textbooks. Classes are nice, but most of what you'll learn (and need to know) in grad school you'll teach yourself. A lot of material you thought in undergrad you'd never use will probably start popping up. There will always be something you don't know, but most of your peers are in the same situation. Don't be afraid to ask questions. Eventually you'll become accustomed to running into material you've never seen before. Reading more textbooks and articles to get up to speed becomes a matter of course.

Graduate-level research also involves competition with your peers. In undergrad, everyone was looking to do the bare minimum of work to get through a class or to get the minimum grade they would settle for. Now you're dealing with professionals, most of whom not only work in this field, but who love it and have a calling for it. They're always working to produce the best, and if you want to get noticed, you must be at the top of your game yourself. Research is a collaborative effort, but there is no glory for second place. In a class, everyone produces the same output for evaluation by a professor. In graduate research, you submit your unique work for evaluation by peers. You are measured by the *new* material you produce, not by the correctness of a uniform product as in class.

Depending on your personality, research is either delightfully or intolerably open-ended. Even when you put together a crisp and clearly defined project proposal, the point of research is to explore. Few research projects offer anything as easy to aim for as a "deliverable." In fact, you and your advisor may not even know if the goal can be achieved at all. That's what research is for! If you truly desire a beginning-and-end, goal-oriented work environment, grad school is not for you. That sort of world is what you find in industry.

Your research will involve many branches and tangents, and most of them will be dead ends or outright failures. It's from the failures, however, that you learn. No one ever learned how to do something right by doing it right the first time, your advisor included. Part of the professional maturation process is seeing where all the branches take you, and storing that experience away for the future. One day you may be faced with similar research problems, perhaps as a professor with your own students, and you'll be able to tap into that long history of dead ends to streamline your work in the present.

Choosing Your Research

Everyone in grad school likes a challenge, but a satisfying challenge must be surmountable. Spinning your wheels on the same project for years breeds resentment and despair, not the sense of accomplishment you came to grad school for. Your graduate research defines who you are professionally and is the deciding factor in your happiness over the next several years. You don't want to get caught on a project you hate, no matter how famous the advisor or prestigious the research group. If you are miserable, you will look back on these prime years as wasted, wondering why you hadn't gone over to another group down the hall and enjoyed yourself. In the end, everyone's M.S. or Ph.D. counts the same, no matter how fancy your experiments or exclusive the journals you publish in. If you want a rewarding experience in grad school, you must choose your research as carefully as you would choose a spouse.

If you have a big-money advisor, you may get stuck doing the research you're funded for. The advisor secures a pot of grant money and then brings you in, like a new employee, to work on that particular project. In this scenario, the grad student doesn't have a lot of control, and if you end up in this situation, use orientations and visits before grad school to find out exactly what you're getting into. Your advisor will have written the grant himself and navigated bureaucracy for years to get his hands on that funding. Grad students come in at the end of the process, when the research finally has to get done. By the time you come into the picture, many details of the project have been established through mutual agreement among collaborators. The philosophy, motivation, and methodology for experimentation have been decided months in advance in the proposal itself. A number of background experiments may have already been performed by someone else to motivate the proposal that's funding you. In fact, much of the research for a proposal may already be done, and the grant money is used to seed new exploratory research to motivate yet another new grant. It is your challenge as the grad student to follow the path specified by your advisor while also making the research your own. An M.S. or Ph.D. is made up of *your* research that *you* have to defend in front of your future peers. You must understand why you are doing particular experiments over others, and why you are doing the research at all.

In contrast, many grad students are able to choose their own research. Often the choice is between a handful of projects your advisor has on the front burner, where each project in isolation may have rigid plans based on the proposed research, but at least you get to choose which of them suits you best. Or, you have the opportunity to research whatever you want, which is more common in theoretical research, and in particular when you have no research funding. A lab with consumables requires cash, and the funding available does not permit research into whatever strikes your fancy. However, if you are not funded by a particular project (that is, you're a teaching assistant or paying your own way) and all you need for research is pencil, paper, and a computer, you could be free to go wherever you want with your research.

As you make a decision, you should keep in mind what you need to graduate. The university imposes demands that you can't control, but your advisor also has rules. Your advisor expects a certain level of scholarship before he will consider letting you defend and graduate. Some advisors are perfectionists and insist on a sublime piece of research for your M.S. or Ph.D. Other advisors make blanket expectations of two or three published journal articles before they allow you to graduate. Advisors run the conceivable gamut of demands. The question is, among the research projects you have to choose from (or to invent), how hard is it to satisfy those expectations?

Your personal goals also merit weight in your decision, thinking back to the reason you came to grad school in the first place. Are you in grad school to change the world? The sentiment is noble, but is it prudent? You don't want to be in grad school forever. Making a big contribution to the field calls for extraordinary effort on your part, and there is high risk that you won't succeed. Some research problems promise to change the world if they're solved, but you may not be able to solve them in the time you have.

Or, you may be in grad school for pragmatic, career-oriented reasons. There's nothing wrong with wanting an alphabet soup after your name to buff up a resume. In that case, aim for the bare minimum to graduate, if your advisor lets you. The bare minimum is still a *lot* of work, but large, earth-shattering projects may not be appropriate if you're looking to get out of grad school in the shortest possible time.

There are two kinds of research: the low-hanging fruit, and everything else. Few grad students pursue low-hanging fruit, even when it is staring them in the face. Low-hanging fruit are old ideas with a new twist. They are the application of new methodologies to an old problem. When new tools become available in your field, you can go back to basics: apply them to models and analyses that you learned in your first year of undergrad, because no one has seen them in this new light before. Genetic algorithms, which were developed by biologists in the 1950s to study evolution, were taken up by inquisitive researchers in aerospace engineering to find more efficient airline schedules. When carbon-dating techniques became available for paleontologists and archaeologists, historians exploited it to create a definitive timeline of pre-history and the ancient world. Classics students had whole new tracts of literature to translate, study, and publish when they shined new-fangled X-rays on ancient scrolls that had melted together over the centuries. When rudimentary electronic calculators were invented, it became possible to compute in seconds the logarithm tables that had once merited a Ph.D. of its own to produce. These were all low-hanging fruit for grad students once upon a time. Merging two disciplines (like X-ray imaging and Latin scholarship) and leveraging new tools and methods can reveal a new world waiting for the astute grad student to snatch up and exploit. With low-hanging fruit, the field is wide open to publish, publish, publish!

If you're looking for low-hanging fruit, broad-spectrum journals are a good place to start. These journals publish articles with far-reaching ideas, whose authors are well-established researchers in their fields and can afford to stick their necks out. Sometimes the authors simply become notable for the frequent publication of their pie-in-the-sky papers. Robert Forward, an aerospace engineer and science fiction author, published many scholarly articles on interstellar travel, fantastical propulsion technologies, and planetary colonization. His work inspired the research of many grad students. Lucky for you, as a nobody just starting out, you can also afford to stick your neck out and pursue some of these hare-brained schemes if you want!

The musings of your advisor and colleagues are also a prime source of low-hanging fruit. Experienced researchers have a million ideas that bubble up over the years, but they simply don't have the time to pursue them all. You might be able to show that an idea is worth pursuing after all.

When you're out of low-hanging fruit, you're left with the barren tree. These are the hoary old research problems, where the fruit has been picked clean. The sparse fruit that remains at the top is the shiniest, but it is also the hardest to reach. On the climb up, there is a risk that you'll fall off the tree a couple of times before you reach the top, if you get there at all. These hard problems have been studied for centuries. Some problems remains persistently unsolved (like, say, the Collatz Conjecture* in mathematics). All of the simple applications have been worked out, and you're left in an obscure corner of the field to make your mark. Imagine in the humanities writing a Ph.D. thesis on Homer's *Iliad*, which has been the subject of scholarship for thousands of years! It would be challenging indeed to say anything new. All of the obvious solutions and the obvious methods to the hard problems have been tried by people much smarter than you. Sometimes, the research itself is *about* proving whether the problem is hard (such as if $P = NP$ in computer science).

Your advisor is the main source of direction for fruit on the barren tree. He knows the material best and knows what could stand to be worked on more. Advisors frequently have pet problems that they recycle for M.S. and Ph.D. degrees over and over again, and they always have a new take on them. The discussion and conclusion sections of journal articles are a good source of direction. After an article has presented its new research, the discussion section talks about what the results mean, how assumptions and methodology could affect the results, and what work remains to be done. The authors are giving you a hint about what you could do to improve or carry on their work (of course, the authors are also probably pursuing it themselves, so the clock is ticking).

Review articles in journals, while not presenting original research, are tasked specifically with summarizing the work that has been done in a field, discussing the gaps in knowledge, and

---

*If you want to burn an afternoon on this maddening problem that sounds easy, here it is: Take any number n greater than 2. If n is even, divide it by 2; if n is odd, multiply it by 3 and add 1. Repeat the process indefinitely. The conjecture states that no matter what number n that you start with, you will *always* eventually reach 1.

suggesting future avenues of research. Also, former grad students in your research group have produced documentation on particular problems far in excess of what appears in journal articles. Every grad student leaves ideas hanging when they graduate. At the end of every thesis you'll find a "Future Work" section. The graduating student, coming up on a thesis submission deadline, wants to get out and justifies all the unfinished work in that last chapter of their thesis. You can pull many great research ideas from there.

When you're climbing the barren tree, you would be well advised not to let the perfect be the enemy of the good. You'll never have the perfect paper. If the case has been made and the results are sound, publish them and move on. It would be wonderful to submit a perfect example of scholarship to a journal, but you can spend your entire life pursuing that goal. If you did somehow manage to achieve it (or something close to it), the odds are high that no one would recognize it anyway. Most people don't read beyond the abstract, figure captions, and conclusions, and history is full of famous and seminal papers that were ignored, ridiculed, or rejected in their time.

Your Academic Plan

Time is precious, and course catalogs change every semester. The most advanced graduate-level classes may be offered only once every two or three years, and missing one could derail your entire graduation timetable. If you want to satisfy academic requirements with a minimum of stress, you need to make a plan and lay out all of your classes for the next few years (preferably for all of grad school).

Before the time comes to register for classes, you should study your department's requirements for graduation. The department website lays out everything you need to know, but the requirements are never straightforward, and you need to make absolutely sure you know what you need to graduate. Most departments offer a grab-bag of courses, often broken up into different sub-fields, of which you must take a fixed number in the proper proportions. Your program may even allow you to count credits from other departments. Study the recipe carefully. Too many students (both grad and undergrad) have been shocked at what they thought was the end of their program, only to discover that they missed one class. Don't let that happen to you. Consult the administrators and staff if you are unsure of what is expected of you.

The most obvious part of the academic requirement is credit hours. The department demands a fixed number of hours to be completed for the M.S. and Ph.D. Not all of those credit hours have to be spent in class. You may be able to use research hours to count towards graduation, but that depends on the department and university. There is a minimum number of credit hours per semester (around 9 hours is typical) to maintain status as a full-time student, and fewer in the summer. Being a full-time student comes in handy to keep the student loan enforcers at bay. When you're not full-time, the loan repayment clock starts ticking!

Part-time students can take as few classes as they want, and as infrequently as they want. This approach is cheaper on a per-semester basis, but part-time students may still be stuck paying the university's exorbitant fees. You should carefully consider whether you need or want to be a full-time student. If you are juggling a job or family at the same time as grad school, full-time status may not be best. There's no sense paying tuition up front to get overloaded with classes that you may not pass.

There are many resources to exploit before you select your classes. Your advisor no doubt will have many suggestions for you, and he may insist on your taking certain classes whether you want to or not. You should take his suggestions with a grain of salt. He may not know you very well yet, and classes that he recommends might be good for some and bad for others, depending on your background. Getting advice from current students and from fellow research group members is a prime way to cut through the uncertainty. They know what classes to avoid, which professors to avoid, and the classes' work loads. Seek out classes relevant to your research, and if you're lucky they also take care of your academic requirements. As time marches on and you start running out of options, it is common practice to take easy classes to polish off those requirements. In undergrad it would look odd for a senior to take an introductory, freshman-level class, but in grad school nobody pays attention to these things. If you need one last class and no time for something challenging, the credits from "graduate-level" introductory calculus count as much as any other, as far as the university is concerned.

You will develop a love-hate relationship with the classes you must take while you do your research. You negotiate your class load with your advisor, but grad students rarely take more than three classes in a semester. The more classes you take, the faster you'll be through with them. If you're in grad school for the long haul, and if your advisor has burdened you with a lot of responsibility in the lab, you may take only one class at a time. You may take no classes at all during crunch times, like when you are preparing for qualifying exams. Your goal is to finish class requirements as quickly as possible, so that you can devote all of your time to research. It is the research, not the classes, that gets you out of grad school.

You should identify early on the course load that you are comfortable with. Four classes per semester will satisfy your requirements quickly, but can you achieve acceptable grades for all of them at the same time? The value of grades in grad school is different from undergrad. At many schools, a grad student must achieve a minimum "B" grade for a class to count towards his or her advanced degree. A "C" grade, which would have been tolerable (if lackluster) in undergrad, is essentially a failing grade in grad school. If the class doesn't count toward your academic requirements, it was all wasted time. Even a "B" in grad school can be perceived as a black mark. Aim for a course load where you are reasonably confident of pulling in an "A" for all or most of your classes.

Are all those classes worth it? Every university sets the number of classes you must take for your graduate degree, and a limited course catalog eventually leaves one feeling that precious time is being lost on pointless academics. Classes can be a thorn in your side, but you can get something out of every class, even with the worst syllabus and the worst professor. You at least encounter new subjects, methods, and techniques, which may not seem useful now, but a few years down the road you may be thankful to have had the exposure. If academic requirements force you into "useless" classes, there's no sense in being resentful. Make the best of it, and get what you can out of the class. As with undergrad, study the syllabus and get a clear understanding of what the professor expects of you, and when he expects it.

Many valuable classes are offered outside your department,

and you may discover some gems in the course catalogs of other departments. You must make sure that classes in other departments count toward your degree, but if the material is relevant to your field and your research, they usually do. There are lots of great faculty teaching in other departments, and you can take advantage of the opportunity to broaden your exposure to other fields. An aerospace engineer can get a lot of use from classes in mechanical engineering and physics, and it never hurts to see how people in other fields view the same problems that you tackle.

Your Research Plan

Just as there are no truly normal families, there is no normal research. Every grad student has a vision of a perfectly stated thesis, a carefully executed regimen of experiments, the masterful publication, and smooth defense. It never goes that way.

Although your department sets out its demands for graduation in black and white (courses, forms, exams), the main ingredient for graduation—your research—has no clear path. As your research begins, you may feel like you have no idea where it's going or how you can get from start to finish. Nonetheless, a rough plan of your research, composed at the very beginning, focuses your efforts and can prevent the aimless melancholy that afflicts your grad-student comrades.

Your research plan may be simple or convoluted, linear or serpentine, depending on the research and the desired degree. At the very start of your grad student career, the research plan doesn't have to be entirely coherent, and it doesn't need to survive long before you compose a new one. But having one at all puts you ahead of the majority of your peers.

As you prepare your research and as you execute it, the literature in journals is key to staying on top of your game. Know the literature, feel the literature, be the literature. Live it and breathe it. You'll encounter seasoned researchers who can quote research papers like Bible verse. The journals are where you'll do the majority of your learning. There's a point you reach very quickly when textbooks fail you, and the only place to expand your knowledge is through reading the literature. Contemporary journal articles are not obligated to provide introductory material (in fact, they are discouraged from it). Rather, they off-load that material to a reference, and you may find yourself tracking references back decades. Once upon a time, I tracked an equation in a 21st century paper back to a German textbook from the 1880s, just to know what a "commonly known" equation was about!

Your research plan should contain some semblance of a timeline. It should reflect how long you want to take for your graduate degree, and that time span should be realistic! You won't go from undergrad to Ph.D. in 3 years, so don't plan on it. Your fellow group members and advisor are guides to estimate how long it takes to finish an M.S. or Ph.D. in the group, although if you ask them directly they probably won't give you a straight answer. You'll have to deduce a timeline from the group's graduation rate.

Timelines can be substantially different for international students and can skew your perception of what a reasonable time is. Depending on the field, it may be very difficult for foreign nationals to get a job in the United States, and international students may stay in grad school 50% longer than their domestic counterparts primarily to preserve their visa. Even if their research is done, it is not too hard to finagle a teaching position for an extra semester or two. They use that extra time to perform the job search, which may be much easier to do at the university than back home.

Your research plan's timeline breaks down the research into goals and subtasks, as best as you can manage. Now is the time to embrace the WAG—the "wild-assed guess." There may be one or two big goals, and there are many subtasks to achieve them. You can assign an estimated time for how long each subtask takes, and account for the probability that you have to repeat some of them. Adding up all the components of your subtasks gives you a feeling for how long the research will take as a whole. You may find that you can afford to pull some tasks out and still get the job done (you don't want to be in grad school for 10 years!), or you may have to add some. Any timeline you compose will be very rough, but it's better than nothing. You'll go down many interesting tangents that may or may not be fruitful. Delays always crop up, and things go wrong. Keeping a constantly updated timeline on hand keeps you informed how much (or whether at all) those delays matter.

Making a timeline of your planned research is one thing, but obeying the timeline is something else entirely. You could simply calculate your timeline. Basing it on your projected research, you break down tasks further and further until you add everything up and get a final date as output. This method makes your research flexible, but it also projects your life in grad school longer than it needs to be. No hard deadline for finishing is imposed, because you let the research itself determine the deadline. You are at the mercy of the research and the capricious forces that affect its progress.

Or, you could outright set a deadline. You choose from the beginning how many years you want to take, and see if you can fit your research into that time frame. You gauge how your effort input and anticipated research output can accommodate the deadline. Setting a deadline is hard to do, especially at the start of grad school. You will probably need your first year just to get a sense of what a reasonable deadline would be.

During your first year or two you may follow more of the first path, setting goals independent of a date. When you become more comfortable in your grad-student role, you will be able to say something more definitive like "I'm going to graduate at the end of next year." A personal chronological goal, as long as it is achievable, is more satisfying psychologically. The graduation process usually takes a semester or two to get in motion, with all of the forms and exams and defenses you have to schedule. Once you make your deadline decision and you set the university's graduation wheels in motion, there is great motivation to finish your research in the time you've allotted yourself.

Time Management

Managing time makes or breaks the sanity of a grad student. At the start of grad school, an infinity of time stretches before you, but at the end of grad school, you wonder where all the time went. Most students enter grad school immediately or shortly after undergrad: they start in their early twenties, when four years seems like a long time, and they finish in their late twenties, when time passes more quickly.

Short-term time management keeps you sane from day to day. The best way to get through each day is to remember that you still need sleep. Grad-school classes should not require many or any all-nighters any more. Being a grad student is more akin to a "job" than undergrad. Many graduate students function on an 8- or 10-hour day, rather than the 36-hour marathons common in undergrad, and if you're producing good work, you might be able to get away with less than an 8-hour day for short stretches. Each grad student lives by his or her own circadian rhythm. Many grad students waltz in at noon and stay until 10 or 11 p.m. Some crazy ones come in at 7 a.m. and leave at 6 p.m.

Unless you have teaching responsibilities or a control-freak advisor breathing down your neck, you can come and go as you please. Many universities have policies that dictate the comings and goings of its paid grad students, who are technically employees of the university. The school may require permission from your advisor to take time off outside of regularly scheduled holiday breaks and specify a minimum number of hours that should be spent in lab. As a salaried worker, however, you are judged by the quantity and quality of your output, not by the number of hours invested. It is uncommon for these rules to be enforced except by the slave-driver and control-freak advisors. For the most part, if you need to take a day off, no one will stop you and no one will care.

Responsibilities in the lab may keep you on a strange schedule, especially if you tend lab animals, which may trap you in lab for long stretches or force you to return at odd hours for short intervals. Usually you can see these issues coming and schedule your life around them. If an ongoing experiment requires your presence from 8 p.m. to midnight, you might not come into work until the next afternoon.

Other than lab responsibilities, the largest demands on your time day-to-day are teaching and group meetings. Teaching responsibilities are conferred from on high. You may have to lecture several times a week, or show up to a professor's lectures; you may have to hold office hours, which you may or may not be allowed to schedule yourself, or show up for other class activities. Most of these time demands are out of your control. Research group meetings happen every week or two, and you might be responsible for presenting the progress of your research at every meeting. Reporting your progress on a deadline forces you to budget your time each day so that you have something to show. You don't want to receive a dressing-down from your advisor!

Long-term time management requires balancing semester- and year-long responsibilities with the daily grind. You must attend a handful of classes every semester. Each syllabus lists when exams are held; if it doesn't, find out from the professor. Knowing ahead of time what day (and what time of day) the exams occur prevents conflicts months down the road: you can control your own research schedule better than the class schedule.

Year-long time commitments also loom large in the life of the grad student. You may have yearly reviews of your progress by the department or research group. Although milestones like qualifying exams are legislated by the university, the department can also keep tabs on your progress by demanding annual reports to your committee. Funding agencies, such as those paying for fellowships and research grants, also want reports. Your advisor may be personally responsible to the funding agencies, and he'll task you with writing up your results.

Professional deadlines are also on your plate. You should keep track of abstract deadlines and event dates for conferences you would consider attending. Abstract deadlines sneak up on you fast, and it is best to avoid frantic abstract-writing sessions the night before the due date, which even seasoned researchers get caught in. A rhythm of research develops in a group coinciding with conferences and their associated deadlines. For example, if your group regularly attends an early-autumn conference, the winter months before is spent preparing an abstract. By the spring, after the abstract is submitted, the research gets into full gear. By the end of the summer the experiments are wrapped up and the conference paper written or poster printed. After the conference, the rest of the fall is spent converting that conference work into a journal article, which gets submitted before Christmas. Rinse and repeat: the next abstract deadline is in only a few months!

There is a dirty secret of time management: research doesn't have to be very time-consuming at all. Although crunch periods do abound—when you're in the office or lab from dawn to dusk (e.g., before quals, prelim, and defense, and before major conference deadlines)—there are large swaths of time when no deadline looms. Productivity in grad school is seldom constant. Instead, you will probably find yourself in a spurt of intense productivity for a couple of months—riding the high of a recent discovery and improved blood sugar levels—and then languish in surrounding time where you do next to nothing, for which you experience intense guilt. This productive-unproductive cycle repeats many times over the grad student's tenure.

Unless you are stuck with a control freak or a slave driver for an advisor, there's no reason to expect you have to work 60 hours a week. No one can keep up that kind of schedule and remain healthy. If you maintain a moderate pace through careful time management, realistic expectations, and a wise choice of research topic, you can have an enjoyable and mostly stress-free time in the lab.

Chapter 6

Funding

Poverty in grad school is a badge of honor. If you haven't had to think twice about an investment in Ramen noodles at some point in your grad-student career, you're missing out on a formative experience: appreciation that you're in grad school for the love of the subject rather than to make money. If you want to start making money right now, science and engineering offer plenty of options in industry for people with bachelor's degrees. With a regular job, you could make a regular salary and avoid years of toiling in indentured servitude towards a more advanced degree. If you pursue an advanced degree, especially a Ph.D., there must be an element of dogged devotion to research and the quest for knowledge that offsets the grinding poverty that comes with being a research or teaching assistant.

Grad students in the sciences and engineering have one advantage over the humanities: the relative abundance of funding, whether from government research agencies, industry, or teaching introductory classes in the department. Research labs require a lot of cash to operate, and labs that have been around for a long time are led by professors with a top-notch reputation and a steady stream of money. This doesn't mean that you'll be paid well, but you will at least be paid.

During the admissions process, each department assesses its ability to fund its graduate students, whether in labs, where students work as research assistants for their advisor, or as teaching assistants in classes. Funding in some disciplines has been flush for so long that many departments will not accept a student unless he or she can be funded. Alas, this policy doesn't apply everywhere. As enrollments go up and down and funding ebbs and flows, some fields simply run out of money. You may be accepted by the university and department, but they may not guarantee funding for you. Certain fields don't attract research dollars any more, and there are only so many fellowships and teaching assistantships to go around.

This chapter looks at the costs of going to grad school and the various ways that you earn your keep, usually as a research assistant (RA), a teaching assistant (TA), or, if you're lucky, on a fellowship. Even though your main goal as a graduate student is doing research, large amounts of your time will be spent doing a job that barely pays the bills.

The Costs

The largest cost of attending graduate school, as with attending undergraduate, is tuition. A semester's tuition these days can go into the tens of thousands of dollars. Private research universities demand a large up-front price that includes many fringe benefits, the same model as a country club. Public universities charge less, but they are simultaneously slaves of the state and the dreaded legislators in the capitol. Public schools make a distinction between in-state and out-of-state students, and a substantial differential in tuition comes with it. Despite the fact that you might move your entire life to become a grad student, leaving behind all official ties to the state you started in, that's usually not enough to qualify for in-state tuition. Unless you get yourself a driver's license, voting registration, bank accounts, and maybe a mortgage in your new state, you'll be stuck paying out-of-state tuition, which could be as pricey as a private school.

Thankfully, funding through your department almost always comes with a tuition waver. When you receive an offer to become an RA or a TA—or if you receive a fellowship through the university—you also get a reprieve from paying thousands in tuition. If a tuition waver is not explicitly mentioned in an offer, call the university and make sure it applies, and get it in writing. Unlike law school or medical school, which seldom offer such wavers (or offer funding of any kind), it is in fact possible to leave grad school debt-free, and whatever debt you might accrue is usually manageable thanks to the employable skills you develop in the sciences and engineering.

Tuition is not the end of the story, however. Universities also charge fees. Every university subjects its students to a potpourri of fees, and every fee is evil. Fees are used as a means to circumvent rises in tuition and discriminate against more expensive majors. Fees are not mentioned in university advertisements, so as they rise, the school can continue to advertise "affordable" tuition. Total fees also tend to be department-specific (that is, there may be some fees for engineering students but not for linguistics students), which makes it very hard to sum the fees that apply to you ahead of time. Nobody knows how much they will actually pay in fees until they've enrolled in the school and committed to pay them. Fees are especially popular at public institutions, which are often restricted by state law on how much they can raise tuition. But fees are fair game, and since fees are not usually covered with a tuition waver, you have to pay them whether you like it or not.

The most common fees are associated with a specific school, college, or department. For example, the Graduate School or the College or Engineering at your university may charge fees only to the students under their umbrella. This extra money keeps the school or college running on top of whatever they get from the university's coffers. There are a lot of extraneous deans and support personnel who expect to be paid.

Resource and "differential" fees are also common. These fees crop up in lab-, equipment-, or technology-intensive disciplines. Engineers require a lot of computing resources to perform their studies, and the computers (and the electricity, and the IT support) must be paid for somehow. Many departments at first try to pay for these resources from their regular budgets, but as funding tightens, fees are imposed to make up the difference. Because fees cause a lot of ruckus, usually they are specified at their inception to be intended for only one purpose (like a differential fee for computers), but the porosity of academic bureaucracy and short institutional memory ensures that that commitment does not last long. Many students (especially the grad students, who actually pay by themselves instead of through their parents) agitate against these new fees, but once they've graduated, the department can plunder the money for whatever they want. A differential fee to pay for technology quickly morphs into a slush fund to pay for colloquium speakers, new secretaries, and professors' salaries.

Of all the thousands of dollars in fees that I paid during my five years in graduate school, perhaps the most odious was the "Graduate Appointment Fee," which you may be charged when you become an RA or a TA or receive a fellowship through the school. The fee is levied to make up for the administrative cost of processing your employment paperwork, regardless of the fact that the administrative staff is already paid for. The school essentially charges you for the privilege of working for them. Depending on your department, that fee can amount to a quarter of your semester salary. And you have to pay that fee every semester!

Not every school has all of these fees, and their amounts vary widely from institution to institution. Fee levels evolve over years, influenced by the school's solvency and by the rapaciousness of its bureaucracy. Some schools may charge little, or waive fees entirely for graduate students, whereas you may encounter schools that charge everything to everyone all the time. When you are considering a graduate institution—where you must make ends meet on your own for five or more years—knowing how much money will flow out of your pocket to the school in fees is as important as knowing how much you're going to be paid.

One cost advantage in graduate school is the precipitous drop in materials costs. As an undergraduate, each class you take requires a bulky $100 textbook that is updated to a new edition so frequently that you can seldom sell it back. Unfortunate souls in the humanities are saddled with hundreds of dollars each semester for dozens of little books, each with their own individual markup. In grad school, the number of classes you take reduces to one, two, or three, and the syllabus becomes specialized enough that no textbooks may be available. Your first year or two, you may shell out for texts on advanced topics, but when classes mirror the level of cutting-edge research, there are no books to turn to. Typically, these classes consist of reading journal articles, which are free through the university, or the professor's notes, which are also free or have a nominal printing cost.

Although it almost goes without saying, your computer is your life line in graduate school, and you should make sure you have the equipment you need to live your life and to do your research.

A well-funded research group may assign you a computer from its technology budget. This computer is not yours, no matter how long you have it or what you do with it. If you have a research-only computer, you are best off using it only for research. The computer is the property of the university, which means that everything on it also belongs to the university. You have no expectation of privacy, and you don't want to depend on someone else's computer for your personal work. If your advisor starts nosing around for progress on your latest journal article, you wouldn't want him discovering an unsavory web history!

For those without flush technology budgets, research is usually done on your personal computer. You have the most control in this situation, but also the most responsibility. All of your years of hard work hang in the balance on a machine that no one else supervises. Getting a nasty virus or a hardware malfunction could destroy all of it, obliterating not only your progress but also your advisor's investment.

If you do research on your own computer, you must back up your work frequently and in multiple places. External hard drives are cheap, and you can copy the contents of your entire computer onto them. Doing this every couple of months will prevent catastrophic losses. Daily backups are also advisable for the work you're doing at the moment. Every day of graduate school I carried a small flash drive that held all of my research on it. At the end of every day (sometimes more often), I updated the thumb drive with all of the new work I had done and carried it with me everywhere I went. If I was going out, whether out to a bar or out of town, I also took the thumb drive with me, and I never left my computer and thumb drive in the same place for extended periods. If there was a fire, or an earthquake, or an alien invasion, I didn't want both repositories of data lost in the same disaster. Leaving an external hard drive in a secure place that you don't visit often—and carrying your freshly backed-up thumb drive with you at all times—guards against all but the most extraordinary failures of technology.

Money in Research

Young professors seek their first drips of funding—the driving
factor to achieve tenure—as early as possible, but getting started
in the research business is as hard as anywhere else. Even in this
day and age, most of the money is still funneled through the old
boys' network. Funding agencies award money to the established
researchers with a track record of delivering journal articles that
make the funders look good; the established researchers gain *still
more* notoriety until they themselves are invited to become reviewers for proposals at the same funding agencies; these reviewers know all of their reliable and established colleagues for whom
the agencies' funding is most suited; and eventually reviewer and
researcher switch places in the eternal revolving door.

Many agencies have tried to disassemble the old boys' network
by making grant proposals anonymous, but any researcher worth
his salt can make himself known through the content of the grant
proposal itself (especially when a list of references suspiciously
has all the same names). Just as a young professional is stymied
when every job solicitation demands "5 years experience" for applicants, the young faculty member has no easy way to get on
the ride when the only professors being funded are those already
"with a track-record of successfully funded projects."

But honestly, what is a funding agency to do? These agencies are seldom run by actual researchers or scientists; they're run
from the top by political bureaucrats, often appointed to the job
as a reward for their skills in raising campaign contributions and
squeezing the right palms. If university politics seem daunting,
imagine having to referee grant proposals at NSF or NASA, where
real politics are involved. If you're hired as a grant reviewer and
recommend canceling the wrong project or funding one in the
wrong state, you could have angry senators calling you at all hours
and condemning you on national news. Can you blame them for
funding the least controversial projects they can? Should we be
surprised that they hesitate to take a chance on a young and un-
proven professor, when the director of the agency would have to
explain to *Congress* how he screwed up if that professor burns
through a million dollars in grants with nothing to show for it?

Many grad students are disheartened that so many avenues
of research (invariably your own) cannot attract funding, but the

most successful post docs and professors are those who understand the political realities of what is "fundable" and, when the money is flowing, how to keep it flowing. Funding agencies have charters, vision statements, and missions, which are composed after careful review by both researchers and politicians. When these guide posts are in place, the money goes where the mission statement says it should go, not necessarily where it is most needed. Tenure-track faculty cannot pick a field of research and wait for a funding agency to solicit proposals on that topic. It will never happen. A professor must look at all of the solicitations already out there and figure out how to contort his or her skills, resources, and publications to apply to each of them.

When first starting out, a young professor may in fact know very little about how to execute the research they are proposing to do; they need the start-up funding to get their career going. Eventually a few publications come out, and hopefully that pedigree is strong enough to attract a slightly bigger grant that again the professor may or may not know how to execute. Once you have tenure, and if you're clever enough to make friends in high places, you'll then be able to have funding agencies write solicitations *for* you by making the requirements of the proposal so specific that no one but you could ever satisfy them (yes, this definitely *does* happen, and quite often!).

You may be under the impression that a grant proposal seeks funding to perform the research in the proposal. In fact, by the time you get to the grant-writing stage, you're probably halfway done with the research already. Funding agencies are risk-averse and will not fund a proposal that has a chance of outright failure, which is the case when you propose research that you've never done before. The reviewers must be assured that lots of "preliminary results" and "previous publications" exist indicating that the proposal's avenue of research is a sure thing. However, the only way to know that is if the proposed experiments have already been done. If you haven't finished much of the proposed research by the time you write the proposal, you won't be funded. So where do you get the money to do the "preliminary" experiments so you can write the grant? From your previous grant, of course!

Research Assistant

If your advisor knows how to play the game and is well funded, you may escape the clutches of teaching purgatory and be paid through a research grant as a research assistant, or RA. The RA is a paid position through your research group to do research and nothing but. When your advisor applies for grants, he assigns a hefty portion of the budget to paying for a stable of grad students to actually do the work. When a professor has money of his own linked to a grant with his name on it, he has enormous freedom to hire as he sees fit. When the professor is seeking new hires to work on a grant, you may be interviewed just as you would for a regular job: you meet with the professor and other grad students, tour the lab, and discuss your skills and interests. If you are offered a position, you are asked to commit to a full-length degree program, possibly on that one and only project. If your research interests and the grant funding align, you are the most fortunate of grad students: you are paid to do the work that you would have done regardless of funding.

An RA is like a full-time job, but you only get paid half-time for it. Paid research positions at a university are perhaps the last surviving remnant of indentured servitude in the civilized world. You are expected to show up in lab in excess of 40 hours per week (while technically only paid for 20) and perform an endless series of repetitive or menial tasks that primarily benefit a superior who is not actually accountable whether you succeed or not. If you want to leave the program early (breaking your verbal agreement with your advisor), a particularly vindictive PI could make it difficult or impossible to go to any other research group by refusing to offer a recommendation. Your reputation in general would suffer because an abrupt departure from a group could brand you as unreliable. This apprenticeship can last a half-decade or more, after which you have nothing tangible to show for it and your newly acquired skills may or may not make you employable. This arrangement sounds like something from the seventeenth century, not the modern world.

All the money going into your pocket comes from a grant that has been processed, scrubbed, laundered, and skimmed through a layer cake of university bureaucracy. What you actually get paid is a small fraction of what the budget allocates for your salary, and that allocation is a microscopic sliver of a whole grant. A sizable chunk of the grant money goes into paying your advisor's salary. If your advisor is a PI on a large grant, his entire salary may come out of the pot. This arrangement is expected in academia, and if you do some sleuthing you may find that your department pays only half of the salaries of the faculty it employs. Being paid through a grant, the professor can often take whatever percentage he wants, rather than what the university might have otherwise paid him. Covering his own salary and funding a half-dozen grad students makes him very popular with the department, improving tenure prospects and gaining benefits like a reduced (or non-existent) class load. Even if the grant isn't large enough to pay an entire salary, the professor may skim off the top to pay for work in the summer, when the university may not pay him at all.

The largest line-item for a research grant, however, has nothing to do with research. It's a word called "overhead." Every university requires a certain percentage of every grant be paid directly to the school's coffers, never to be seen or heard from again. These overhead costs go into paying for the processing of the grant and legal services, for the facilities (like the electricity and water bills of your fancy lab), for administration of the grant (like setting up RA positions and the associated work in human resources), for covering tuition waivers, and other bureaucratic expenses. This overhead percentage can be higher than 50% of the entire grant! On top of the university's pound of flesh, the professor can send some funds directly to his department as additional overhead. This extra money covers department-specific costs and facilities, like secretarial support, and also helps as a bribe to smooth reviews at committee meetings and for promotion decisions.

The overhead and hidden costs don't affect the RA directly, because they are handled by the PI when he composes the grant. However, it is instructive to be aware of exactly how much you cost the funding agency, which is usually a government entity spending taxpayer (i.e., your) dollars. If your salary is a measly $20,000 per year, then when you account for 50% university overhead, 10% department overhead, and a fraction for the professor's salary, the allocation for your salary was actually upwards of $100,000!

Teaching Assistant

The most common source of funding outside of research grants is being a teaching assistant, or TA. In departments where research funding is sparse, such as mathematics and statistics, nearly all of the graduate students may be TAs, and even where you have funding through your advisor, some departments require a semester or two of TA work for the sake of experience.

Graduate schools have an unspoken goal of creating more academics, for whom teaching is, in theory, their primary job. To create freshly minted Ph.D.'s who go on to illustrious careers at other universities, the graduate school wants you to be exposed to the art and craft of teaching before you leave, so that you know what you're getting into if you go into academia. If you have no funding and must be a TA, you'll get a lot more experience than you bargained for.

TAs supplement the instruction of undergraduate and graduate courses. As an undergraduate you probably complained about the TAs, about the time it took to get homework graded, about the syllabus and the exams, about the timing and quantity of office hours. Now you see how it really works, and it isn't pretty. The deficiencies experienced by students are not maliciously imposed by instructors, but rather are symptoms of a system that barely holds together at all. Except for perhaps the most established classes with ancient syllabi and the most organized professors, teaching a class is an exercise in choreographed pandemonium. Sometimes this pandemonium isn't controlled at all, and only sheer luck keeps students from seeing through the façade.

Professors have many other responsibilities that demand their time and attention in addition to classes, and they often push classes down the ladder of priority. Lectures must be prepared and delivered, homework collected and graded, labs proctored, exams written and administered, weepy students consoled, and grades submitted to the registrar. Teaching a class is a lot of work. It is hardly any wonder that professors foist as much of the grunt work onto the TAs as they can get away with. What work the TAs can't do, the professors leave to the last minute. The syllabus may change because of the professor's mood. Exams or homework may be postponed suddenly because of a conference coming up. Print-outs for the students may come hot off the copy machine only minutes before they're needed in class. The students are the customers of this disorganized labor. They see only the end product, not the chaos that coalesces at the last minute into a problem set or PowerPoint lecture.

Most TA positions that you can hold are in your own department, where you have the most experience, and you may have even taken the classes yourself. The more familiar you are with the material, the easier your job is. For new graduate students, especially those new to the university, the department assigns classes to TAs at its own discretion. Fresh grad students start with undergraduate classes, where the material is basic and the curriculum more universal: introductory chemistry is more or less the same from university to university, whereas upper level classes may be influenced more by the particular character of your department. TAs are assigned graduate-level classes only after they've taken them, and often at the request of the professor. Your advisor, who teaches two classes or so per semester, may prefer to have his own students for TAs. That way, there is no external force making demands on your time. If your advisor is also your boss as a TA, he has the power to balance the time you put into your TA and research responsibilities.

Many departments cannot guarantee funding as a TA, and you come into graduate school without a funding source at all. Before you take out loans, you should consider seeking a TA position in another department. Scientists and engineers have a broad set of skills that apply to many departments, especially when it comes to teaching introductory courses. Departments such as physics and math have hordes of undergraduates taking required courses, and there may not be enough TAs to cover them all. Mechanical engineers have the skills to teach introductory physics, and chemists can cover introductory calculus. Your skills cover many disciplines, possibly more than you realize. If you are looking for funding, browsing through the departments and programs on the university's website may give you several ideas. You can contact staff in each department and see if they are hiring. The worst they can do is say no. Some departments may even have an open application process for its excess TA positions. Foreign language departments are also an excellent source of funding. If you speak another language fluently, or if English is not your native language, there may be a place for you as a TA for introductory language classes.

Aside from foreign language classes, classroom instruction in the United States is performed in English, a fact that seems to escape many grad students from abroad. If you must instruct in English, then you must be able to speak English, and at a high enough level that you can effectively communicate complicated and technical material to the uninitiated. *Basic conversational English is insufficient.* Students, both graduate and undergraduate, are challenged by new concepts and must concentrate very hard to understand new material. It is a gross disservice to burden them further with the challenge of deciphering grammatically ambiguous and phonetically unintelligible instruction. If your English is poor, take advantage of your university's English-as-a-Second-Language (ESL) programs and build a strong technical vocabulary before you set foot in a classroom.

Responsibilities of a TA

The exact responsibilities and commitments of a TA vary widely from class to class and from professor to professor, but a handful of common themes appear in all TA jobs. A TA is usually a half-time position. Your official commitment is 20 hours per week, but your actual commitment will vary. Some TA jobs consistently require 20 hours each week, and others have fluctuating demands from week to week.

The reason for half-time, as opposed to full-time or quarter-time, is a function of the number of students in each class, university policy, and the tax code. Often a tuition remission kicks in only at the half-time level, and if enrollment in some classes is low, you may be assigned two classes for the same job (where each class counts as a quarter-time commitment). Graduate students are never assigned full-time work, which brings with it a number of legal obligations for the university, including medical benefits and vacation time. They prefer you to remain an indentured servant, with few demands from the state to ensure your well-being, and half-time is enough to keep you flush in Ramen noodles.

The most common responsibility for any TA is grading, lots and lots of grading: grading homework and problem sets, grading pre-lab exercises, grading post-lab reports, grading projects, grading exams. Most grading time in science and engineering is consumed by problem sets and by other weekly (or semi-weekly) assignments, like lab reports. The professor usually has an answer key ready, but it is often the TA's responsibility to write up the solutions distributed to students after the grading is done. That way you gain familiarity with the homework by copying it out yourself. Some sadistic advisors have been known to have their TAs actually do the homework themselves, to keep them sharp on the fundamentals.

The most important thing about your grading responsibilities: do not fall behind! In a class of 50 students, where each homework has 10 problems, that's 500 individual items that need to be graded. If each problem takes 30 seconds to grade, that's four hours of work. Every week, another problem set piles on, and quickly you can find yourself drowning, losing entire weekends to make up for lost time. All the while, you irritate the professors and the students, who want the material graded and returned. What's worse, if you have three or four problem sets to grade in one weekend, you may end up giving your students short shrift as you rush to get the grading done. Your best bet is to keep your grading responsibilities at a low, constant level throughout the week.

Supervising labs is also a common TA job, requiring a lot of hands-on attention. Supervising lab means many dull hours of watching undergrads do experiments and making sure they don't stray from the assignment, damage expensive equipment, or blow up the building. Undergraduates have little practical experience in a lab, and probably no experience with experimental design or data interpretation. The assigned lab projects attempt, of course, to gradually teach these skills, but the learning process is messy. Undergrads do mind boggling things in the lab. They inadvertently mix hazardous (or explosive!) chemicals, over- or under-measure reagents, use the wrong resistors and inductors on circuit boards, fail to plug in the oscilloscope, and everything in between. These flubs come from inexperience, although to the TA it feels like a spiteful assault on your sanity. In the lab, the TA must be the attentive mother hen, preventing the chicks from straying too close to the foxhole. It is a frustrating and thankless job, but somebody has to do it, and it certainly won't be the professor.

TAs also hold office hours, specially blocked periods of time when the students come to you for help. The number of office hours you hold is probably mandated by the university, department, or professor, but *when* you hold them is often up to you. Although you may be required to hold 5 or 6 hours per week, you can't practically hold them at 6 a.m. on a Monday, or at 8 p.m. on a Saturday, and if you did, you'd be obligated to show up regardless of whether any students do. Furthermore, office hours shouldn't reinforce bad student habits. If hours are scheduled on the night before or the morning of homework due dates, students are guaranteed to scramble in with no time to spare. A mix of hours in the morning and afternoon accommodates students with wide-ranging schedules, and adding hours around exam time relieves the pressure on them and you.

Students at office hours come with questions on homework, projects, and upcoming exams, and they do anything they can to get the answers out of you. They want you to give them the answer for the homework, or exactly what will be on an exam, and you must resist the clever ways they try to weasel the information out of you. You can guide them, and offer advice on study habits, methodology, and time management, but resist the urge to give them an answer. They would leave satisfied, but they won't have learned anything.

Students mostly come to your office hours when something has gone wrong, and at the last minute. If homework is due tomorrow, you are guaranteed to have students showing up at your door today. Students who haven't even started the homework come to you with terror in their eyes, having realized they can't whip up a solution in an hour. They could have started the homework days ago, but Comrade Smirnoff and Herr Jägermeister took priority, and now they are paying the price. Somehow, though, the lesson is seldom learned, and the cycle continues every week until the end of the semester.

If it's not for homework help, the students badger you over an incorrect grade that you assigned. The errors are rarely significant statistically; their final grade in the class won't change. Students with a 95% on an exam are the most likely to come to you over a 1-point grading mistake. Without question these errors should be corrected, but the intensity of the students' indignation at such mistakes never ceases to amaze.

In some disciplines, office hours are replaced by a recitation section, a sort of mini-class or lecture that the entire class (or a subset of a large class) attends. In recitation sections, students bring homework questions with them and the TA helps the group as a whole through the problems. The format can be TA-led or student-led, typically at the discretion of the TA. Larger-scale lectures are usually not the responsibility of the TA. That is the professor's job. However, a professor heading out of town for a conference may give the TA the job for a lecture or two.

For all your responsibilities as a TA, you should also know what you're responsibilities are *not*. You are not the professor. It is not *your* class, and you are not responsible for setting its policies regarding how final grades are assigned (although you may assist in the actual assignment of the grades), when and how the students should be examined (you shouldn't be writing the exams or homework, except under the supervision of the professor), or how to structure the syllabus. There are some scenarios where advanced grad students with lots of TA experience are "promoted" to being an instructor who more or less runs the class. If you are in that position you will know it, and even then much of the syllabus, lecture content, and homework assignments are handed to you from a legacy archive. If a professor tries to hand off this responsibility to you, you should push back. The tasks of writing a syllabus and assigning grades is a jealously guarded rite of the professoriate, and you have no business taking it on. If you do, you now make *yourself* liable for the outcome of the class. If something goes wrong, you expose yourself to the danger of the professor throwing you under the bus because you unwisely meddled in class affairs that weren't part of your job.

Teaching assistants are also neither psychologists nor parents. Your office hours are for assisting students in the execution of their academic obligations to a class, such as completing homework and preparing for exams. Personal conversation is inevitable, especially if you're already friends with the students, but you are not a psychiatrist. You cannot indulge a student for an hour listening to dorm-room drama that led to late homework. You cannot (and should not) offer personal advice beyond what is useful for class. That is, advice on study habits is encouraged, but advice on dumping a boyfriend is not. If a student is suffering from an extraordinary crisis—personal or otherwise—that affects his or her ability to do work for the class, you should send the student to the professor, who has the authority to act on it.

The Joy of Teaching?

They say working in retail would be great if it weren't for the customers. As a TA, the students are your customers, and after a while you may feel the same way. If you have never taught before, it may come as a shock to discover how unruly even the most advanced students can be, and how hard they try to do the bare minimum to get by. You'll think back to your own experience in school and be confident that you were better, that you were more diligent and neatly filed each problem set on time, but rest assured, you were just as bad as they are.

New TAs get the introductory classes, which means teaching freshmen. If you've made it into grad school, it's a sign that you're a dedicated and experienced student. You've been in school for so long that you've absorbed the collegiate way of thinking and problem solving into your bones. The first-year students have not. They find not only the course material difficult, but even the way of thinking about problems—which you take as second nature— is foreign to them. Freshmen are new to college. Overwhelmed by the experience, after only a week or two they become over-fed, over-partied, over-sexed, and hung over. They are unaccustomed to the college workload and haven't yet learned how to budget their time effectively. A grad student would find their work positively trivial, but a four- or five-class schedule is oppressive for kids fresh out of high school.

My first week as a graduate student and as a grad TA, I proctored a computer programming lab for freshmen engineers. After a morning of group work on a variety of problems, students were individually assigned a quiz to test what they had learned in the lab: they had to write a program that calculated the sum of the first 10 integers. This problem is trivial, and its solution was obvious to me based solely on the content of the day's lab. Instead, the class was gripped with terror. A buzz of nervous mumbling spread through the classroom and nearly all of the students struggled to the last second to complete this unexceptional task. The students not only had found the assignment extremely difficult (and, therefore, "unfair"), they were downright indignant that it had been assigned at all, as I had not taught them the specific task of summing integers. Students rushed to the professor to complain about me and the unfair quiz (as though I had anything to do with it). More than a few tears were shed in the professor's office by high-school valedictorians shocked to find an "F" on their nearly blank quiz sheets.

In high school, rote memorization is the path to success. From French vocabulary to lists of integrals, the high school student is very good at squeezing a finite amount of data into his or her brain for a short amount of time, just enough to pass an Advanced Placement exam. In college, the tables are turned. All of the facts and figures—supposedly learned in high school—are now treated as a *resource* to build new knowledge and to solve problems. College courses do not teach solutions to classes of problems, as in high school. *College teaches the skills that leverage knowledge to find solutions.* This is an intimidating and alien way of learning, if all you've ever known from high school was memorization.

My students learned a lesson about life in college that day. College may be the first place where they actually try their hardest and still fail, without remorse from the faculty. In high school, students have been coddled with inflated grades, and "honors students" possess a fragile balloon of self-confidence that college pops without mercy at the first opportunity. However, I myself learned a bigger lesson that day. The person I was at 18 was not the same person I was at 22, on the other side of an entire college experience, and being a TA involves a lot more than reciting course material.

Once students get past the freshman culture shock, work as a TA shifts from coddling young minds to indulging disinterested ones. Your students are still over-sexed, over-partied, and hung over, but they've learned the ropes and know how to game the system to get the grades they will settle for. Sophomores and juniors are in the most challenging years in technical disciplines. The course material is demanding, and there is no end yet in sight. These are the years of all-nighters and group homework sessions. Students show up to your morning office hours disheveled and exhausted, probably not having been to bed in a day or two. Alas, your job as TA isn't much easier. The material is indeed challenging, and odds are you don't remember a lot of it yourself. Everyone remembers the basics, and everyone remembers the advanced material that their research focuses on. The material in the middle is a minefield of forgotten definitions, hazy derivations, and seldom-used jargon, and you're responsible for keeping these insomniac students on the straight and narrow!

Chronologically, you are closest to the seniors and you can likely sympathize with them the most. Seniors are fully acclimated to college life. They take the most advanced classes, but have learned how to handle the workload and manage their time, even if that still involves being up all night. The seniors' main priority is to graduate. Senioritis is settling in, and some may already have jobs lined up after graduation. They may do only the bare minimum to pass, graduate, and start earning a paycheck. The experience and detachment of the seniors may make life for the TA easier, but the advanced nature of the classes puts on added pressure that you know your stuff.

One of the more dismaying aspects of teaching undergraduates is how many of them don't care about their work. Their parents are paying for university, and many have prioritized the booze-cruise aspects of college life. This is by no means a large proportion of the students, but it is more than just a few. You're in grad school because you love your subject enough to take a vow of poverty and study it for another half-decade, but nearly all undergraduates are in college because "that's what you do." They are not worrying about their future career or their intellectual growth. It's either college or the real world. Inevitably, this leads to a fraction of students who, quite frankly, shouldn't be in college at all, and some fraction of that fraction will be your students as a TA. It is unrealistic to expect these students, and any students, really, to care about the course material as much as you do.

You will also be surprised at the number of students who do poorly or fail entirely. In many cases, the TA's role in introductory science or engineering courses is that of hospice nurse, alleviating the students' pain as much as possible until the semester is over and a low (but hopefully passing) grade is recorded. I have known many students who were exceptionally devoted, made a strong effort in their studies, came to office hours, sought out tutoring and extra help, and still failed. It was disheartening to watch this drama play out. Some people are not cut out for the work demanded in a technical curriculum. This is not a moral judgment, but an overwhelming empirical fact. We all have strengths and weaknesses, and TAs encounter many students whose weaknesses are in technical areas. The best the TA can do is put in a good word when the grades are finally assigned.

Having other grad students as your students is a different experience. After you've taken a class, you might be assigned as its TA the very next semester, provided you got a high enough grade to qualify. Grad students tend to be more professional in their studies, having made the decision themselves to be in grad school. There may be less fuss and whining directed to TAs from other grad students, but this is not necessarily the rule. In grad school, where research is the key to graduation for most degrees, classes are a necessary evil. Grad students may need to achieve a minimum grade to stay in their program, but the absolute value of grades is not nearly as important as it is in undergrad. The advanced degree itself is the credential coming out of grad school, as opposed to a GPA, and grad students may contribute even less effort to a class than your undergrad students. This lack of incentive is exacerbated if you work in a grad program that institutionally inflates grad-student grades to prevent excessive attrition.

A subset of students in your class are the long-distance students. Universities are finding it increasingly profitable to offer courses and entire degrees via the Internet, and you may be responsible as a TA for students pursuing an advanced degree a thousand miles away. Distance students submit course materials online, and make use of office hours either by email or phone. These students have day jobs, and classes are paid for by their employer. Aside from the inconvenience of a specialized mode of interaction (the Internet, as opposed to in person), these students are usually easy work for a TA. They already have experience, having spent some years on the job, and have a strong work ethic. Their employer probably requires a minimum grade for tuition reimbursement, so the student has a strong motivation to keep those grades up. If there were a chance the student couldn't pass a class, they wouldn't take it in the first place.

Your boss, the course or lab instructor, is an interesting animal. This person may be a full-time professor, or a mere postdoc. Professors and post-docs, especially at large institutions, are in their position primarily because of their research ability, not their teaching or communication skills, and there is no guarantee

that they have any talent at organizing a class. Most are not cognizant of their own idiosyncrasies and quirks. In a research group
these quirks must be tolerated by only a dozen people, whereas in
class, hundreds may suffer under the capricious demands of blue-
ink-only homework assignments, three-whole punched project reports, and assigned seats in lecture. Unfortunately, no one can
ever call them on their unreasonable or anti-social behavior. All
one can do is suffer through it until the end of the semester. The
instructor assigns the TA all the work he or she doesn't want to
do, which is most of it. The clerical work is the job of the TA, as
is keeping track of the homework, recording the grades, and issu-
ing messages to the class. At universities that prioritize research
over teaching (which is most of them) you may end up with some
instructors who just don't care. If they hate teaching and no one
can force them to make an effort, they will do the bare minimum
to qualify for doing their "job" and leave the rest to the TA.

Although most professors, especially well-funded ones, are im-
mune to the disapproval of students, TAs are usually not. Many
schools have students rate teaching assistants at the end of the
semester as they do professors, and these ratings can have a major impact on your future employment. TAs are a dime a dozen
in most departments. The supply of people seeking TA positions
always exceeds the departments' demands, so they can afford to
dump the unpopular or ineffective TAs no matter how badly they
need the job. Low ratings over several semesters create a pattern
that justifies not renewing your employment in the future. High
ratings may get you more pay, and consistently high ratings may
bump you up to teaching higher-level classes.

When you venture forth to your first class or two as a TA, there
is some behavior to avoid. A large part of your role as a TA is judg-
ing students, either through grading homework, grading exams,
enforcing syllabus rules, or dealing with policy infractions. It is
easy to be too harsh and follow the strict letter of the law, or be too
lenient and empathize with a student's every crisis. You must find
a happy medium between the "good" cop and "bad" cop, where
the students respect you and your authority but don't hate you for
it. Remember, the students are not personally invested in the material the way you are. You are the crazy one devoting a career to
this stuff.

If you're a pushover, the students *will* walk all over you. It is human nature to manipulate people in power to the maximum extent possible. If you're too easy or nice, you'll get all of the students' attention as they bypass the other TAs. This sucks up all of your time, and the students expend more effort finding ways around their work than actually doing it. On the other hand, if you're a monster, your reviews at the very least will suffer, and passive-aggressive undergraduates can make your life miserable. Undergrads one day become grad students, employees, and employers. It does you no good to make enemies. Every class has rules, but it is important to remember the human dimension to the educational process.

The last word to say is that the TA is not the students' friend. This is especially the case with undergraduate students. You must maintain a professional distance, lest the students begin to believe that a buddy-buddy relationship with the TA confers special privileges. A high-school calculus teacher of mine once opined, "Don't crack a smile before Thanksgiving." When the teacher-student dynamic is established, future interaction can be more relaxed. You're in grad school now, and you should have a grad-school social life. Undergrad is behind you. Don't make the mistake of trying to hold onto (or recapture) your free-wheeling undergrad life by bar-hopping with students.

In the same vein, don't sleep with or get romantically involved with your students. Some universities prohibit it internally, and in some jurisdictions this is prohibited by law. The frequent interaction between students and TAs is a prime incubator for romantic interest, but it can also be a source of manipulation. Romantic dalliances with students are an insoluble conflict of interest, and one needn't search far to find a story of a student trying to trade sexual favors for better grades.

Fellowships

With a TA position, you have to teach to get paid, and you still have to do research to graduate. With an RA, you get paid to do research, but you have to do the research that the grant is paying for. The brass ring for all grad students is the fellowship, where you get paid by a benevolent entity to research whatever you want in whatever fashion you please. A fellowship is free money, with tenures as short as a semester or as long as four years. You get paid for doing your research, not a grant's and not even necessarily your professor's. Having a fellowship gives you freedom not only in your research but also in how you are managed. Fellowship students are popular for advisors, because they are free students for the research group and one fewer person the professor has to worry about feeding. A student with a fellowship has usually been through a rigorous selection process, so having that fellowship is a signal to advisors and future employers that they've been "vetted" by an outside authority. Advisors know that if a student is talented enough to win a fellowship, they will almost certainly do fine in their research group and the risk is low that they will need a lot of hand-holding during their grad-student career.

A research fellowship is free money, but the amount of free money depends on the granting institution. Your fellowship can cover tuition, fees, materials (e.g., books), and travel, and pay a stipend, or any combination thereof. Covering tuition is the basic definition of a fellowship. If only part of tuition were covered, or if it didn't cover tuition at all, you'd usually call it a grant. Fees may or may not be covered, and getting travel paid for is rare, although some high-profile fellowships include a small travel budget for a conference or two.

The stipend is your salary, and may or may not exceed what you would have been paid as a TA. In fact, some multi-year fellowships require that you work a semester or two as a TA to gain experience. If you're considering becoming a professor yourself, keep in mind that a fellowship can inhibit gaining experience in teaching or interning in industry.

Fellowships can also make your taxes complicated. Fellowships administered through the university are probably handled like any other job, with a W-2 and other tax forms, but that's not always the case. If you're paid directly by the awarding agency, you may have to pay self-employment taxes and estimated quarterly taxes. All the ins and outs of your responsibilities to Uncle Sam are complicated, and the university will not help you. The school will not provide tax advice to anybody. If the tax situation associated with your fellowship is unclear, you should get yourself an accountant. You do have to pay for it, but with an accountant handling all the details, it only takes five minutes to do your taxes.

Many fellowships are awarded internally through the university, and sometimes they are awarded long before you even get there. To recruit attractive grad students, some departments tap internal fellowships to pay for them. While most students get letters with offers of TAs or RAs, there are a few blessed souls handed the free money on account of their impressive scholastic achievements. Before you matriculate, you should consult the website of the university's graduate school and see what fellowships are available to apply for. After you arrive, you may have the opportunity to apply for fellowships that require status as a current student to be eligible. Once you're at the university in person, it is easier to track down these funding options. Administrative staff in your department are a great resource for finding out what opportunities are available.

The most famous fellowships in the sciences and engineering are funded by the government. The National Science Foundation is the great grand-daddy of graduate fellowships, handing out about a thousand cushy fellowships every year across all fields. Other agencies give out fellowships in their particular bailiwicks: NASA, the Department of Homeland Security, the National Institutes of Health, the Department of Energy, and Department of Defense. Most federally funded fellowships require U.S. citizenship, and you must also beware the fine print: some fellowships, especially those from defense agencies, may require you to work for a U.S. government agency during the summers and after graduation. That doesn't mean you have to join the military, but you would have to, say, work in a national lab for a few years after you get your degree. This clause limits your choices after graduation, but on the bright side, the fellowship agency is also guaranteeing employment. Not a bad deal.

Privately funded fellowships are available from a range of nonprofit groups, although full tuition payments with a stipend are not necessarily as easy to come by as with the public fellowships. A lot of private fellowships are more "scholarship" sized, covering a semester or just travel. These fellowships are typically focused around the quirks of a particular bequest (e.g., only for Irish-Americans named "O'Malley," or only for students who are ambidexterous), but the restrictions are not always made public. One famous fellowship (which shall remain nameless) is particularly biased in favor of applicants with good rags-to-riches stories, although this is not advertised. Other fellowships are segmented by technical field, sex, race, or other arbitrary measures.

Competition for every fellowship is fierce, but you have no excuse not to apply for every one of them. Fellowship applications seldom require more than a couple of essays, a transcript, and a handful of recommendation letters. At the expense of a half-day's work, you line up for a chance at financial security for the next several years. When you account for the tuition and fee payments, stipend, and other fringe benefits over a three-year tenure, an NSF fellowship is worth about $200,000. That's a great deal for six pages of essay-writing. Even if there's only a five percent chance of winning a top-of-the-line fellowship, you would be a fool not to give it a shot.

Loans

When all else fails, you can turn to loans. Your friends in medical school and law school already probably live on their student loans, but it is notably less common in the sciences in engineering, thanks to the general availability of TAs and other funding. Nonetheless, not everybody gets paid for their entire time in grad school, and the bank may be the only place to go (aside from getting a part-time job at the record store, of course).

If you're in grad school for your M.S., a loan may not be the worst option in the world. You'll only take on a couple of years of loans at most, and most jobs in science and engineering offer a comfortable pay scale after your M.S. A two-year debt load may be manageable. If you can take out loans just to cover tuition and get a temporary job to pay the rent and bills, you would be even better off.

For a Ph.D., the loan scenario is more precarious. Many students are not funded their first year, but have a good chance of getting funding in subsequent years, in which case a first-year loan for your Ph.D. may be reasonable. Whereas an M.S. has a more definite timeline, your Ph.D. could go from 4 to 7 years, or more. If you're taking out $30,000 in loans each year for grad school, that's more than $100,000 in final debt load! It is critical that you find other sources of funding. You would need to make a doctor or lawyer's salary to comfortably manage debts that size. Doing an entire Ph.D. on loans is the monetary equivalent of buying a house. Do you think you would be able to start paying off a mortgage right out of grad school? If not, then you may not want to "buy" that house-sized Ph.D. by starting grad school in the first place.

You may have already been through the loan process as an undergrad, but odds are high your parents handled the finer details. When you take on grad student debt, it is entirely yours, and you have to know everything about the obligation you commit to. Loans come in many different flavors—federal, private, subsidized, unsubsidized—and many of them cannot be discharged in bankruptcy. Know when those loans come due! As long as you are a full-time student, you don't need to pay, but interest continues to accrue and the rates aren't low!

If you don't sign up for classes in the summer, you may cease legally to be a full-time student, in which case the debt agency starts the repayment clock. You don't want to get caught unawares half-way through your Ph.D. and discover you have to start making payments during a summer session.

Chapter 7

Going to a Conference

Before universities were centers of scientific research, they were religious institutions that educated young nobles and the future clergy. Wealthy pupils learned Latin, philosophy, theology, and rhetoric: all the skills necessary for a medieval lord or abbot. Investigation into the natural sciences, on the other hand, was focused around private societies, where like-minded, inquisitive minds met to discuss the experiments and findings of its members. Seminars were held at the societies' meetings, during which members presented papers on their projects and reported discoveries from voyages around the world. These societies covered every topic imaginable, from astronomy to chemistry to horticulture, sponsored expeditions to remote parts of the globe, and promoted the scientific interests of its members. As a notable example, in the 18th century, the Royal Society of London dispatched Captain James Cook to Tahiti to observe a rare astronomical event; in the process, Cook mapped the coastlines of New Zealand and Australia and claimed the lands for Great Britain. Charles Darwin, whose voyage on the H.M.S. *Beagle* led to the theories of evolution and natural selection, was a member of the Geological Society of London. These intellectual societies birthed the tradition of the academic conference that we know today.

Why Attend a Conference?

Working in the comfort of your lab is half of your responsibilities as a researcher. You fulfill the rest by attending a conference, which exposes your research to the community at large and offers the opportunity to interact with your peers. The cycle of research depends on peer review, and you can get it nowhere else with such volume and candor as at a conference. Interaction with a critical community forces you to polish (and own up to) all of your results, whose wrinkles and blemishes become all the more obvious under collegial scrutiny, and by the time you are done, you return to the lab with a broadened perspective and ideas for new routes of investigation.

Generically, a conference is a gathering of a few dozen to a thousand or more researchers who report on the progress of their ongoing work and solicit input from the community. They present their research orally (or, commonly today, on a poster) and submit papers that document their results. Although some people attend a conference to spectate or network, a grad student doesn't get sent to a conference to be a tourist. You'll be there to present your research.

Exposure is an essential component of your grad-student career, especially if you expect to continue on to an academic career, where the conference attendees constitute your future lifelong colleagues. Your physical presence is surprisingly powerful, sometimes more powerful than a written record. Many people don't pay attention to written literature beyond the authors, title, and abstract, unless they want to reproduce your results, but moseying about a conference frequently leads to serendipitous visits to presentations on unfamiliar topics. The conference is your chance to get across the content of your hard work to a wide audience in easily digestible chunks. An impressive presentation sticks in the mind more indelibly than impersonal words on a page.

Personalizing research by interacting with colleagues fosters an open-minded temperament. It is not uncommon to become so engrossed in research that you critique others' work only through the lens of your own interests and biases. You find yourself reading papers and wondering how the authors could have neglected this or that, how they could assert such and such claim, or how they could make daring assumptions that you feel undermine the validity of their argument. This attitude often takes hold at the start of graduate-level research, when you are full of enthusiasm but short on experience. After you meet these authors in person, you can appreciate their personalities, their quirks, and their priorities. Although you may still disagree with their approach or their claims, you have a better sense for what motivates other researchers to pursue a methodology different from your own. What for you is a fascinating subject worthy of a Ph.D. is for others a nagging distraction best dismissed with a convenient choice of assumptions. They have their own dissertations or tenure to think of. Knowing where others come from chills the hot-headed, knee-jerk reaction to attack research that doesn't approach the world your way.

Unfortunately, even in the ostensibly enlightened academic world, advancement is more about who you know than what you know, and conferences help you build a professional network that lasts for your entire career. The people in your research community should know your face, and likewise you want to put faces on the authors whose papers you read. The contacts you make at a conference are indispensable. Having met someone in person, their likelihood of helping you out increases many-fold, even if you only speak to them briefly (like sitting at the same table at the conference banquet). People are more inclined to trust others whom they've met before and had a chance to measure. How much time would you give to help someone whom you've only talked to on the phone? Meeting that person at a conference puts the two of you in a professional context as members of a guild, who are inclined to help each other. Once you're on the inside, you might be able to get your hands on hardware or software, or leverage brainpower, wisdom, and experience that your research group might not have on hand. Conference attendees themselves may not even be the most valuable contacts you make, but their networks are. You may not meet the exact person you hoped to talk to, but if you get the card of a prominent researcher, you can bet that he or she knows plenty of the right people to get you in touch with.

This network is also crucial for the end of your grad-student career, when you begin the dreaded job search. The time for job applications is the time to pull out all those business cards and leverage your contacts for all they're worth. The people you've met at conferences may very well end up being the people who interview you for a job. Without question they'll know if their company or institution is hiring and, if not, who *is* hiring. If you can hand your resume over to a real human being who knows you, you're leaps and bounds ahead of others applying to a job solicitation cold.

Communication skills are critical in any career, and participating in conferences boosts those skills both on and off the dais. A good communicator really does get ahead faster. If you project a confident personality, with a solid head on your shoulders and a firm grasp of technical material, people are much more likely to talk to you, to work with you, and to assign you more responsibility. At your first conference or two you may be very nervous and feel awkward, but the projection of confidence with your peers gets your foot in the door. Real confidence comes later, with experience.

If you present a paper at the conference, you also get the chance to build your skills in public speaking, a task that terrifies many people. You must overcome this fear, and the best way is with practice. If you are an eloquent public speaker, people are interested in you regardless of the material you present. Even at an academic conference, people attend talks to be entertained. A poor speaker embarrasses not only himself, but also the audience. Watching an ill-prepared and halting presentation makes an audience member uncomfortable—not to mention bored—and desperate to escape, whereas an expert speaker lulls the audience into a heady state of mind. When your audience is happy, they are more receptive to your arguments and absorb more of the content you present (especially important if you want to wring research dollars out of them someday).

That same public presentation introduces you to the uneasy task of defending your research. Many people are naturally defensive when they or their hard work are challenged. It is unnerving to have a roomful of smart minds picking apart what you devoted so much time to, and still more disheartening when they inevitably pick up on a few inconsistencies. Processing constructive criticism gracefully—and remaining unflappable in the face of a rude or unprofessional critic—is the hallmark of a mature researcher. The advancement of research depends on critique and collaboration, and you can't take the criticism personally. This environment keeps you on your toes. Through the conference and presentation settings, you solicit ideas and suggestions from your peers, occasionally they point out errors (hopefully minor!), and the commentary refines your work before it ends up in a journal.

Choosing the Right Conference

Given all of the points that argue you *should* go to a conference, it is time to prepare yourself for one, and the first step is identifying the right conference to attend. Although it may seem obvious, it is worth emphasizing that you should find conferences that cover your topic area of research. It's a waste of time and money to attend a conference where no one will understand what you present. Unfortunately, I have seen many researchers choose entirely inappropriate conferences for their presentations, motivated by a desire for exposure. Large, high-profile conferences lure you with promises of A-list researchers and funding agencies in attendance, but the conference still has to be the right fit for *you*. Funding agencies don't fund what they don't understand (or more importantly, what's not in their mission statement).

You can identify the appropriate conferences by following the lead of your own research group. If colleagues in your group attend the same conferences year after year, it is a good bet that you should show up to those conferences yourself. No doubt your advisor will make you go anyway! The conference attendees will recognize your group and your advisor's name, and with that reputation at your back, it is substantially easier to socialize and to build your network. A classic and effective conversation starter is "My advisor is Professor Whoever."

If you are looking beyond your comfort zone, you should check out who else in your field is attending a conference that interests you. The papers of colleagues in other groups can tell you what conferences they visit and what they do there. If those are the people you want to get in contact with, the conference may be a good bet. Selection of a conference by strategically perusing the attendee list is a wise tactic, especially if you're doing research in an area that is new to your group.

The "right" conference may also be affected by other factors, such as funding and geography. My former research group makes a pilgrimage to one particular conference every year. One year it was in Honolulu, and the next in Pittsburgh. The Honolulu conference was popular, but it was also expensive to reach. My group had limited funding, and I ended up presenting other grad students' papers because not everyone was able to go. The following year in Pittsburgh, more grad students attended the conference, and it also attracted a set of researchers from the local area that normally would not have come. If the business of your research is focused, say, in the Pacific Northwest, then more interesting and well-connected people will attend a conference held in Seattle than Topeka.

With these points in mind, you've selected a conference. You remembered to register for the conference, didn't you? Be sure to do that as early as possible: last-minute registration is outrageously expensive!

The Abstract

Your first interaction as a conference attendee occurs months before the conference itself. You must submit an abstract of your research, in which you describe your research, your goals, and your results (and why they're important) in a few hundred words at most. The conference's organizing committee selects which papers to accept, which to demote to posters, and which to reject outright, and this short abstract is all the opportunity you have to impress them. Wading through abstracts is a dull job that one cannot easily persuade busy faculty to perform, so the abstract deadline is usually 6–8 months before the conference, to account for a procrastinating conference committee.

Reporting on your research so far in advance is intimidating. Almost certainly your research is not done by the abstract deadline, or anywhere near it. In some cases, the research may barely be started. This long lead time and the incompleteness of your research is not a deal-breaker for getting to the conference. It's one of the many dances you must learn as a grad student. I once submitted an abstract that was about 80% research plan, not having any idea what the final results would actually be, and frontloaded it with discussion of the other 20% and plenty of journal references. The abstract was accepted. I was a seasoned graduate student when I made that daring submission (I was still uneasy about it) and had a relatively good feel for the most likely results. Nonetheless, you don't want to turn into the boy who cried wolf. Frequent withdrawals from conferences because of jumping the gun with your abstracts create a bad reputation.

Your abstract is limited to a few hundred words, so you must make your point clearly and concisely. The abstract is no time to teach anyone new material, and introductions should be kept to a minimum. I also have one suggestion that may not be popular with seasoned academics: make it catchy. Your title and short abstract are all the conference attendees have to determine if you are worth their time and attention. Would you be more likely to attend a talk entitled "The Effect of Variable Mean Free Path on the Diffusion of Randomly Distributed Particles" or one called "A Mathematical Model for the Zombie Apocalypse"? Both titles apply to the same talk, but I know which one I'd choose (and yes, I have seen mathematicians give conference presentations on the spread of zombie infections). A bland title and incomprehensibly dense abstract—lamentably the norm—attracts only the most die-hard colleagues.

The abstract deadline is the conference's first deadline, and it is a hard deadline indeed! Organizing a conference involves securing a venue, reserving blocks of rooms at a hotel, ordering catering, renting equipment, and a million things that must be ordered far in advance. The number of submitted abstracts locks in the scale of the conference for the organizers, and if you miss the deadline, you probably won't be allowed to submit at all. There is nothing more annoying to conference planners than having to accommodate exceptions to the rules, and frequently they won't.

A few weeks after the deadline (or even as long as two months), you hear back from the conference with its verdict. Hopefully, your abstract is accepted in some form. The conference decides if they want your material presented as a full paper or as a poster. The paper involves a stand-up presentation to an audience, and the written paper is archived in the conference proceedings. With a poster you stand by a glossy printout and chat about your work to interested passers-by (although you may still have the opportunity to submit a written paper as well). As you might expect, the oral presentation, with its dedicated time slot and audience, is more desirable than the poster. Some smaller conferences don't have poster sessions at all and give everyone the chance to present a full paper. These conferences are commonly divided into many small sessions with a few dozen audience members at each talk, as opposed to larger conferences that may have only one or a handful of huge plenary sessions.

Building a Conference Strategy

In the interim before the conference, you work feverishly to get useful results and to complete your research. You also have to budget time to write a paper or design a poster, which always takes longer than you expect. Sometimes the paper must be submitted a month or more before the conference; sometimes it comes after. Don't wait until the last minute to start writing. It may not be going into a journal, but lots of people may reference your conference paper in the future, and it should be as polished as possible. Conference papers tend to have technical, "nuts-and-bolts" material in them, the sort of content that other researchers need to reproduce your results. Readers appreciate a complete report on your methods and results that they can follow and that doesn't abound with compositional errors of haste.

In the last few weeks before the conference, the program is released. The conference program contains the schedule of the sessions and presentations, sometimes a list of attendees, and, for some conferences, a list of booths and tables (for companies marketing their products). This program is the key to planning your conference strategy. More presentations will interest you than you can attend, and reading the abstracts in the program helps you prioritize. You can mark where you want to go for each session and build a schedule. It is best to plan ahead in the comfort of your lab rather than scramble between sessions figuring out where to go next.

Besides planning your tour of conference presentations, it is valuable to plan whom you want to meet and why. Even if a list of attendees is not available, the authors of the papers and posters printed in the program will reveal who most of them are, and your advisor and colleagues can give you a heads-up on who else is likely to be there. Meeting people is the first step to building your network, and you need a strategy for the people you meet. It is tempting to go after famous people (it never hurts to have powerful friends), but if you have nothing to say to them it is not worth the trouble. Approaching a well-known researcher or businessman at a conference is thrilling, but once you've suppressed the tendency to be star-struck, it becomes increasingly awkward when you have nothing to say except small talk. Instead, write down ahead of time who you want to meet at the conference and what you want from them.

Making Your Poster

The *content* of your poster is what excites you. It is the culmination of a year or more of research, and advertising it to the world is a crowning achievement of sorts. Unfortunately, many posters and presentations are so poorly constructed that the content is lost in a haze of block text, dense equations, and pixelated figures. If you don't prepare the choreography—the user's entire experience at your poster—your visitors' eyes glaze over, ears turn off, and all your work goes unappreciated. This chapter cannot provide a comprehensive guide to making a poster or preparing a presentation. Entire books have been written on the subject. Rather, I address a few of the most important points of good style and highlight common pitfalls, so that with any luck you can leap over the hurdle of making a good first impression.

When making a poster, brevity is the name of the game. You've done a lot of work leading up to this poster, and there is a strong urge, given all of that open space, to squeeze in everything you can. You can't fit everything on it, so don't try. *A poster is not a journal article pasted onto cardboard*, and squeezing in even 70% of your material is both overwhelming for the vastness of content and unfulfilling for its incompleteness. Presentation on a poster is an honor reserved for your juiciest results, which may amount to only 10–20% of your work as a whole, but it's those choice results that you want your visitors to walk away with.

Physically, you can fit only so much material onto a poster's space. The board or sheet is no more than 3-by-4 feet, onto which everything must be included. Before content is added, consider how a visitor will look at the poster. Potential visitors wander the conference without paying attention to anyone in particular. To grab their eye, include the most important text (that is, the title) in large font that is easy to read from at least ten feet away. Print out some sample text on regular sheets of paper and see how tall the text needs to be. Probably two inches at least.

Once you've attracted a visitor, they don't want to hunch over and squint while they read. The rest of the poster text should be legible from at least three feet away, which means fonts about a half-inch tall. Clearly all the text on a poster has to be big, and you won't be able to fit much on the poster after all.

The poster is a backdrop for you, not the other way around. The limited content on the poster is not a bug, it's a feature. The poster cannot stand entirely on its own, and it shouldn't; otherwise, there's no need for you to be there yourself. The poster is a tool for you to refer to and support your conversation. While you talk eye-to-eye with a visitor about your work, you periodically use the poster to point out a choice figure or an illustrative (but short!) equation. The poster should have no block text and no huge equations. No one will read them, and if they did, time is so short they probably wouldn't really understand them. You are there to help them understand.

The content of the poster is the star, and the results may be what excite you, but the poster should be visually attractive as well. You want to draw people to the poster. Bright colors are effective, but they must be a highlight and not the main attraction. Neon orange works as a border, but using it as the background for the entire poster will give visitors a headache. Color requires a subtle touch: too little and the poster resembles boring newsprint, too much and you've got a clown.

Your poster must be organized with a logical flow that follows the conventions of any other advertisement: top-to-bottom and left-to-right. You will be tempted to put highlights in the middle of the poster, but that's not how people read. It's not possible to cue on the poster itself where the reader should start, so you have to account for custom. People expect an abstract and introduction in the top left, which should be mercifully short, a clear representation of the problem. Methods and results come next, in the same order as a journal article. If you organize it correctly, you might be able to get your results in the middle anyway. Discussion and conclusion continue with the top-bottom, left-right flow.

A standard-sized poster has two or three columns. Never make a visitor read text across the poster's entire width. Figures should be clearly labeled (and all axes legible!) with pithy captions that convey everything the reader needs to know. In the end, you should have a poster that, while it may not stand on its own, brings the visitor through the entire tale of your research from beginning to end.

The physical construction of the poster also warrants attention. This poster will be abused from sea to shining sea, carried onto airplanes, stuffed into suitcases, hauled around in taxicabs, rolled and unrolled countless times, and assaulted by pointing conference-goers with greasy hands. You should invest in the highest quality poster possible. It is worth getting a glossy finish to protect the poster from the elements, and heavy paper stock to withstand frequent handling. A cylindrical carton for transportation will save your bacon on many occasions (especially for airplane flights), and in the spirit of always being prepared, having clips and a cheap tripod on hand is invaluable if the conference doesn't provide them or runs out.

Preparing a Presentation

When it comes to presentations, you should avail yourself of the extensive resources out there. Books, articles, and, yes, presentations on this fine art abound. You can find tips on what to wear, where to look, how quickly to speak, what size words you should use, and how to tune your message based on your audience. Much of this advice boils down to checklists of do's and don'ts and treats public speaking as a terrifying chore that one must soldier through. As a graduate student, you can expect to give many public presentations in the years ahead, and as a professor you put on several shows a week in class. Presenting is part of the life of an academic, and it is a skill that can be honed and even relished.

The spoken aspect of a presentation is arguably the most nerve-wracking. It is possible to spend hours preparing your remarks, even memorizing a script for a 30-minute presentation. When I first began giving public presentations as an undergraduate, I lacked confidence and scripted every presentation I gave. That was fine for 15-minute talks, but even in that time frame I inevitably forgot a line, lost my rhythm, and stumbled through the subsequent slide or two. As I got older and gave more presentations, my confidence grew to the point where I no longer needed a script. The experience I gained over time washed away the stage fright, and I no longer needed the crutch of prepared remarks. I knew my material well enough that I could improvise as necessary. Through extensive practice, your speaking will improve.

It is sometimes more important to rehearse what you are *not* going to say in your presentation. No matter how hard you work and no matter how thorough your experiments, controls, and variables, there will be holes in your results. For you, immersed in your research at all times, the holes appear gaping. This is usually not the case, and your advisor can help keep things in perspective. Nonetheless, the shaky or questionable work-arounds that we use to get to our results are not the things you want to air at a public presentation. If you, say, used a less-accepted protocol, didn't actually keep track of the step size on your numerical integrator, or skipped steps in your algebra because you found the result in another paper, keep these things mum. There are a million things everyone does (and you will, too!) that make your work slightly less perfect and less rigorous, even though you know the results won't be affected. These short-cuts and gray areas are a fact of academic life, but it is also inadvisable to volunteer this information. Announcing every insignificant twist and turn you took to get to those results will lead to a question-and-answer (Q&A) session spent defending minutiae instead of discussing your legitimate conclusions. Stick to the facts in your presentation, and let the audience root out details if they want.

Improved speaking comes with experience, but the structural aspects of your presentations, such as what goes onto your slides, can be improved immediately. Many great speakers prepare atrocious slides, and most slides I have seen by all classes of speaker are mediocre at best. Most speakers forget that what they know is not what the audience knows. The audience knows your name, your title, your abstract, and (if you're lucky) something about your topic area. You know charts, graphs, equations, chemical formulae, and the details connecting them. It is easy to throw those details onto slides with great excitement and forget that much of it is "inside baseball" that won't elicit a reaction. The conference presentation is your chance to get the big-picture story through to the audience, and the slides should reflect that goal.

Slides illustrate, not educate. Like posters, they complement what you have to say, and they shouldn't say it all. If your presentation could be given without your being there, then your slides have too much information. People absorb new knowledge slowly, and you cannot bombard them with new material all at once, and not in the short time before you move on to the next slide. Some people prefer to watch you while you talk, others enjoy the eye candy of a slide, and it is your responsibility to make sure that everyone walks away with the bottom line.

Your conference presentation is an advertisement for your research and your paper, not a full-scale colloquium. Trying to squeeze everything in overburdens the audience, and teaching introductory material is an inefficient use of your precious stage time (not to mention that it is rude to teach anything at a conference of your peers). Keep the content to the bottom line, and bring those points home frequently so that the audience doesn't have to do any more work than necessary. Draw the conclusions for them.

Everyone knows you worked hard. No one cares. Everyone works hard, and there's no need to draw attention to it. There are some occasions where the difficulty of your work warrants a mention, especially if you are outlining a tricky methodology you want others to adopt. The most common whining amounts to "it took me hours to solve this differential equation..." Merit is not assigned based on effort, and the young grad students who complain about the complexity of their work appear childish. Rather, it is classy if you downplay the amount of work you did. If you see or hear the famous phrase "after some algebra," it is a tongue-in-cheek way of saying "this took an enormous amount of effort, and I don't recommend you try it yourself!"

Perhaps the single most important rule for slide composition is: NO block text! This rule is also the most frequently broken. This is a presentation, not a report. People read at different speeds, and there simply isn't enough time for them to read and comprehend a whole slide of text. If you read the lines off the slide, there's no reason for you to be there. You might as well have emailed everyone your presentation for perusal at their leisure. Worse, if what you say differs from the block text, the audience will pay attention to only one thing, you or the slide, and absorb neither.

Slide inflation is another affliction of many a presentation. If you only cover the highlights to advertise your paper, you should only need a few slides. A wise rule of thumb is 90 seconds per slide. Discussing a slide always takes longer than you expect, especially when you veer off on a tangent. I have seen colleagues come into a 20-minute slot at a conference with 50 slides, and I ask myself if these people gave any thought at all to how that math could work out. At 90 seconds per slide, a 20-minute presentation should be 13 or 14 slides, including your title slide. Don't make a 35-slide presentation and hope that you can get through it. You can't. You'll rudely eat into the next presenter's time. If 14 slides sounds tight, it should. Being able to edit, edit, edit is a skill. The audience wants to do as little work as possible, so give them as little work as possible by providing only the material most necessary to tell your story. The rest is fluff, and you can stuff it into the paper.

Slide-transition mishaps are the stuff of legend. Advanced presentation-building programs like PowerPoint and Keynote offer an impressive array of transitions (fades, dissolves, wipes, push and cover, bars and stripes) and come with or without sound effects. Animations are a tempting siren during the construction of your presentation, but like the Sirens of Greek myth, they will destroy you. Everyone has a vision of their ideal presentation, which flows at a perfect pace and in dramatic fashion from slide to slide, punctuated by flashy transitions and sound effects. In reality, it is impossible to maintain a narration such that animated transitions are anything but a distraction. Interruptions, questions, and tangents drive you off script, and the momentum of a perfect presentation slips away. In the confusion you forget a few of the transitions, which pass by awkwardly and possibly with a jingle. If you have to go back to a slide during the Q&A, you must progress again through these transitions one by one, amplifying the embarrassment of transitions that didn't go well. Except in the most controlled circumstances, animations, transitions, and sounds are best avoided.

Unless you're a mathematician, math and equations have no business appearing in your presentation, except for those that are absolutely essential. All the math you have done leading up to your paper is truly *your* math. It was probably hard for your own

Presentation Temptations...

Don't include block text
Don't read text aloud straight off a slide
Don't include slide-transition animations or sounds
Don't include complicated equations
Don't include illegible, pixelated graphs
Don't depend on color
Don't forget to include backup slides
Don't rely on default format and font settings in PowerPoint

advisor to follow during research meetings, so imagine how hopeless it is for conference attendees to understand. Include only key equations on your slides, of the sort that illustrate the story you're trying to tell. If the equations are incidental to the point you're making, leave them out. If you do include an equation, you must define all of the variables, explain every term in the equations, and highlight key elements to keep the audience focused on what's important.

Graphs and plots are an excellent way to convey a lot of meaning in a small and attractive package. Graphs and plots are also an excellent way to confuse your audience. Plots are most effective when they are at their simplest and require the least amount of deciphering, and there are many paths to follow so you don't distress your listeners. One way to simplify plots is to use grayscale only. Shades of gray sound horribly restraining, especially in this day and age of fancy projector technology, but I have found from experience that there is a high probability that the projector you're assigned has a malfunctioning color. Projectors break down frequently, and one or two broken color lamps is a common ailment. When the green lamp burns out and all of your plots had green curves, your presentation becomes much more challenging with blank slides! It is also worth noting that as many as 20% of all men (and fewer women) suffer from some form of color blindness. Going with black-and-white plots is an easy way to head off both mechanical and biological malfunction, and if a plot is so complicated that you need color, it's worth considering if your plot is too complicated in the first place. If you must include color, keep it to no more than 3 or 4 colors, and use primary colors for maximum contrast. I once encountered an author who presented a plot with lines in dark blue, dark green, and dark purple, which looked so alike that the author's references to "the blue line" were useless.

Hazy or pixelated graphs with tiny font are a common sin in presentations. All axes in a plot must be legible. Far too many speakers begin such a slide with: "Well, you can't actually read the plot, but the trend is..." If you can't read the plot, why did you include it? The listener should be able to read the axes and other text on the graph from the back of the room without straining. Even if you explain what the axes are plotting, the audience members won't remember, and once they've forgotten, you lose all hope of their absorbing the slide's take-away. Graphs with easy-to-read fonts and axes allow the listener to remind him or herself what's going on while you describe the content and the bottom line. Before you give the presentation, project it at home or in a classroom and see if you can read all the material from 20–30 feet away. If not, the plots should be re-done to make them legible.

As you compose your presentation, you will anticipate questions that require more detail than the presentation proper can provide. This is where you can include backup slides, which are, in a way, the antithesis of the commentary given so far. You are limited to one slide every 90 seconds or so in the presentation, but during the Q&A, it can be very helpful to have extra, detailed slides stacked at the end. No one sees these slides unless they stay for the Q&A, so the backups can be as voluminous and complicated as you want. Your 15-slide main presentation might be supported by 30–40 backup slides with lots of detail and equations. Odds are you won't use more than one or two backup slides, but if prompted you have carte-blanche to go into whatever detail is necessary to answer the question. It is important, however, to know your backup slides as well as your main slides. Even during the Q&A, time is precious, and you don't want to waste it searching through disorganized backup slides.

One brief note on style: the default settings on your favorite presentation-making software are not necessarily the best settings. I have found it unwise to use a pure white background for slides with black text. The white background reflects strongly against the projection screen and is taxing on eyes in a darkened room. A duller grey for a background is more appropriate with black text.

Also, there are more fonts out there than Arial and Times New Roman. Both of those fonts are adequate, but presentation after presentation in the default font becomes monotonous. While you should avoid loud and oversized fonts, using a slightly different font from everyone else can make a presentation pop.

Before You Leave

A number of tasks remain before you can get on the road and make your way to the conference. Reservations for transportation should be made with plenty of time in advance, and plan to arrive a day early (that is, the day before the first sessions of the whole conference, not just the day before your presentation), thereby hedging against travel snafus. These days, it's best to assume that there will be a delay of some kind, especially if you're flying. You're a grad student: you're neither busy nor important enough to fly in only on the day you present. Arriving a day early gives you 24 hours to get to your destination by hook or by crook, even if your bus breaks down and you have to hitchhike the rest of the way.

Business cards are a useful accessory to have on hand. These cards may not be appropriate for everyone, depending on your level of graduate study, but if you're a Ph.D. candidate, you should definitely have them. It is usually possible to acquire business cards through your department at the university, but even if you can't, you should print some out on your own. Business cards with your name and contact info are available cheap online (a few tens of dollars for hundreds of cards), and you'll be very glad to have them when you're meeting all these new people at the conference.

Next, print your materials and handouts. If you're presenting a poster, obviously this must be printed out at the local copy shop (or the university's reproduction facility) before you leave. In general, it's best to go for high-resolution glossy print with a protective case. It's worth the cost: this poster should last a long time. You'll show it many times to the public, use it for recruiting to your research group, and possibly bring it to more than one conference. You should also have a few copies of the paper accompanying your poster or presentation, if you've written one. It's embarrassing if someone asks for a copy and all you can do is promise to email them. Under most circumstances, either you'll forget to send the email or, if you do send it, it won't get read.

If you're giving a full-scale presentation, there are other details to take care of. Presumably, the presentation is in a digital format. Chalkboards and transparencies at conferences are all but extinct. Often, you already will have sent a copy of your presentation electronically to the chair of your session (more on that later). Nonetheless, you should email *yourself* copies of your presentation, in multiple formats. A presentation format like PowerPoint is platform-dependent, and innumerable conference presentations have been ruined by formatting errors on an unfamiliar operating system. Send yourself (and the session chair) a copy of the presentation in a universal format, like PDF, and save yourself last-minute headaches. In addition to the backup electronic copies, print out a full-color hard copy of the presentation. If all else fails, you can use the print-out with a document camera or improvise in some other way. Lastly, put electronic copies of your presentation onto a thumb drive that you bring to the conference. The conference presentation is the highlight of your trip, and all of this redundancy will pay off in case something goes wrong.

When packing your luggage, you'll have to make the proper choice of attire. Acceptable clothing is discipline-specific in many cases, and some might argue that science tends to be less formal than engineering, and academia overall less formal than industry. However, in my experience, the level of formality is determined mostly by age and rank. People who need to appear well-dressed (like assistant professors looking to make a name in the community for themselves, or undergrads trying to swim in the deep end) wear formal attire, and those who don't (like tenured professors enjoying life in the ivory tower) wear whatever is comfortable. Dress is also region-specific: conferences in Boston lean towards formal, whereas in southern California you'll find conference-goers in sandals and shorts! The conference is not the time to express yourself. A conference is for career advancement, and conformity is the norm. Go light on the piercings, jewelry, and body markings, and suppress the mohawks and other distracting dos. When in doubt, dress business casual, and men should always bring along a tie just in case.

The Social Calendar

Conferences are full of social events, and the amount of networking to do can be overwhelming. The best way to keep from drowning is by sticking to the plan you made before you came to the conference. Who do you want (or need) to talk to? You can use social events to run down that checklist.

Receptions are prime networking time. Usually there is one the night before the conference starts (another reason to arrive a day early). The crowds are smaller at this reception, and because there's not much else to do, there also is less time-pressure to get through a conversation. The two-minute elevator pitch can be saved for the session breaks during the conference itself. Larger conferences with lots of corporate sponsors sometimes have receptions every night, and it's worth enjoying these events. Even if you don't do much schmoozing, there's plenty of food to go around.

Every conference has a "gala" dinner or a banquet. This is a catered affair in the evening and is seldom included with the registration fee, so you'll need to pay extra (during online registration months ago) to get a ticket. The banquet room is filled with tables that seat 6–8 people, and seats are not assigned, except for a few reserved VIP tables (and as a lowly grad student, you don't get to sit there). As scary as it is, sit with people you don't know and work on building your network. If you're the timid type, pick an empty table and let strangers fill in around you. The dinner event is an easy venue to meet new people. After the introductions are over, the conversation has a slower dynamic and there is less pressure to maintain conversation. During the day's session breaks, you have to think up things to say in one-on-one conversations that you initiate, but at the banquet you can always retreat to a glass of water or bread during a lull.

Alcohol consumption at a conference is a hairy subject. The banquet may serve wine, or you may have received a couple of drink tickets for the cash bar. Conferences are not dry affairs, and many attendees spend their time carousing with buddies they haven't seen since last year's conference. Obviously, moderation is the name of the game when you're with people you don't know. On the other hand, it is a not uncommon tradition to enjoy a bit of excess with colleagues you know and trust (if you drink at all, that is). Beware, however, that you don't overdo it. Returning to a conference (or worse, giving a presentation) while hung-over is no treat. I know from experience.

If a conference is held at an exotic location or a tourist spot, excursions planned by the conference committee are common, although they do cost extra. The excursions are another excellent opportunity to network in a low-stress environment. Set out on your own, too. By no means is it necessary to stay sequestered in the conference venue. I once attended a conference in Honolulu, where the attendance supposedly was 1,400. I never saw that many people in the conference center, and I didn't see much of that conference myself!

Conference Etiquette

Conferences are broken up into sessions, during which several people present in succession. There could be multiple sessions going on simultaneously, or one large plenary session. With simultaneous sessions, several smallish rooms are prepared identically with space for a few dozen audience members. The more technical the conference, the more likely the multiple-session format. Only a handful of attendees are interested in one tiny corner of research, and the rooms are kept small to save space and make the speaker feel better (who wants to present to a mostly empty room?). During a conference with one plenary session, a ballroom is filled with rows of tables and chairs, and at the front of the room is a dais where speakers do their presenting. Plenary sessions offer exposure to a large number of people, but also increase anonymity: both speaker and audience are physically and psychologically separated by a stage. The theatrics of the plenary make collaborative interaction difficult.

Attending talks involves etiquette that many people fail to observe. You should always go to the talks of your fellow research group members. It is both common courtesy and provides moral support, and a large turnout by your research group looks good to the community, growing your group's professional footprint. Similarly, try to attend talks of groups that you collaborate with, are affiliated with, or are related to yours by subject area. It is gracious to show respect by listening to your colleagues' work, it is prudent to listen to your colleagues and keep up with what they are doing, and it is politically expedient to show interest in groups or individuals that you want to work with in the future.

Being a good audience member is a frequently neglected virtue. Crinkling candy wrappers is a common sin during a presentation. Hotels search far and wide for candy with the loudest wrappers and stock the conference candy bowls accordingly. You should also suppress your coughs and other bodily functions. Clearing a tickle in the throat once is forgivable, but a persistent cough, a sneezing fit, or labored breathing is distracting, and you should step out until you have yourself under control again.

While the speaker is putting on his or her show, it is polite to think up a question. Even if your question is rudimentary, anything is better than hearing crickets at the end of a presentation. It is satisfying as a speaker when your audience has questions, and asking a question yourself can gin up good will socially.

Each session (although not each talk) is separated by a break of 15 minutes or so. This break is more than just free time to nosh on treats at the snack table. This is premium schmoozing time. Approach the presenters you've watched and introduce yourself, ask more questions, and build a rapport. Get as many business cards as you can, and give out as many as you can! You can also use breaks to visit conference booths, if there are any. Talking to industry folks illuminates what's going on outside of academia. They usually have free stuff, too. The break is also the only appropriate time, if you must, to check your email, make phone calls, and attend to text messages.

Showing Off Your Poster

When the time comes to show off your own work, there's a lot of work to be done. First, let's consider if you're presenting a poster. Many conferences have specially designated poster time, which simplifies life substantially when it comes to budgeting your time at the conference: you always know where you're supposed to be. Other conferences have informal "poster time" during the breaks between sessions, an unfortunate arrangement that often leads to aisles of unmanned posters. The cardinal rule of presenting your poster: stand by your poster during all poster times. This *is* what

you're here for, after all, and you don't want to lose any opportunity to advertise your work. There will be lots of empty time
when no one is around, but you don't want to be absent when
someone does come by. If you're with other people from your research group (or from your project), it might be acceptable for one
of you at a time to check out other posters, but try to maximize the
manning of your poster, and never leave it unattended.

Don't be timid with your poster. The poster session is your
only time to shine, so attract all of the attention you can. Take care
not just to stare at someone who glances at your poster and then
starts to move on. *Engage* each visitor who comes near your poster.
Avoid asking "Do you have any questions?" They haven't even
read your poster yet. How could they have questions? Instead,
you will have a more productive interaction if *you* ask pointed
questions rather than waiting for the visitor to say something. Introduce yourself, ask about what the visitor researches, where he
or she is from, how often he or she comes to the conference, or
other bits of small talk. Eventually, you segue into the material
on your poster. Your poster should be an aide for conversation,
rather than a standalone report. The report is what you have all
those copies of your paper for. And of course you handed one to
each visitor, plus one of your business cards.

Giving Your Own Talk

If you're giving a full presentation, there are many steps in the
process. On the morning of your presentation, there is usually a
speakers' breakfast or some kind of gathering for the day's speakers. At this meeting, you meet your session chair and the other
speakers. Although you will have already sent the session chair an
electronic copy of your presentation (probably prompted by a request a few weeks ago), you should have your flash drive with you,
just in case. The chair often brings a laptop to the meeting and up-
loads the files for speakers who weren't as responsible as you. It
is also wise to have a written bio ready, with which the chair introduces you to the audience. A few lines about yourself, your
educational pedigree, and who you work for (i.e., your advisor)
are sufficient. At this brief morning meeting, the chair describes
how he or she plans to conduct the session and the presentations:

whose computer will be used for the presentations (the presenters' or the chair's) and how the chair plans to handle question-and-answer time.

This early-morning meeting of session speakers is also excellent networking time, even though it is early and you haven't had your coffee. Sessions are usually grouped by theme, and it's likely that the people in your session are closely related to you academically. Introduce yourself to everyone, and spark up some conversation. At one conference I attended, I met a pair of distinguished (i.e., nearly retired) engineers at my session's speaker breakfast and we chatted for some time about my work, graduation, and impending job search. The conversation was cordial, but nothing to write home about. A few months later when interviewing for a job at those engineers' own company, I found out that they had praised me to my would-be boss, completely unprompted. Praise from those engineers no doubt contributed to my being offered a position. You never know who you're going to meet at a conference, or when, or how chance encounters may pan out in the months and years down the road.

When it comes time for your session later in the day, arrive promptly, so the chair doesn't worry, and plan to remain in the room for the entire session. If you're not the first presenter in the session, now is a good time to reconnoiter. The uncertainty in giving a presentation—such as who is going to control your slides and where you should stand—is sometimes more nerve-wracking than the presentation itself. You can use this time before your talk to keep an eye out for how things will proceed: where to stand, whether there is a microphone at a podium or if you'll use a clip-on, where the laser pointer is, and so on.

For your own talk, the most important thing is to calm down. Don't worry about how many people there are (whether a lot or a few), or who they are. Timidity embarrasses the audience, so speak loudly, carefully, slowly, and confidently. All presentations are a form of manipulation, and you will be well-served to use your boldest tones and impress your audience, regardless of the content of your presentation. After speaking confidently so many times, you *actually* start to feel confident. A confident orator can make a grocery list into a stirring speech, and you should be able make a year's worth of hard research at least as entertaining.

A few words on laser pointer etiquette are in order. It's a laser pointer, not a laser paintbrush. Innumerable presentations have brought audiences to the brink of seasickness with a red dot swaying to and fro, dragging our eyes in circles until we've lost all sense of a slide's content. If you must use a laser pointer (I actually prefer an analog pointer myself, like a dowel, knitting needle, or rabbit ears from an old television set), then *point* with it. Do not swirl it around. If something on a slide needs to be circled, keep the circle tight and the motion slow. If you swirl in large, random circles, no one knows what you're trying to emphasize and you make the audience motion sick.

Your pointing etiquette should be as well-rehearsed as the rest of your presentation: plan on what you need to illuminate with your pointer. Don't improvise with a pointer any more than you are willing to with your words. A profound lesson of laser-pointer courtesy to keep in mind: *if you don't need to point at something, then don't!* Many people feel compelled to point at something—anything—while talking, but this absent-minded highlighting of material serves only to confuse your audience. With great laser-pointing power comes great responsibility. Just because you have the pointer doesn't mean you have to use it.

At the end of your presentation comes the Q&A session. The session chair usually leads the Q&A, although a more timid chair might leave you to call on people yourself. Composure is the name of the game during the Q&A. Some folks pontificate like Congressmen when called on, and it's best to smile and let them carry on until they get to their actual question. A challenge in the Q&A is staying on topic and addressing the questioner's concern, so be sure to understand the question before you try to answer it. Some people will be very critical, and that's all right. You did come to the conference to get critiqued, after all. Rather, you mustn't let anyone bait you into an argument, or to fluster and bully you to prove their point. Many people have no idea how their tone or language come across. Don't freak out if someone is rude or hostile. Now is the time to learn not to take critique of your work personally.

The volume of questions you receive can mean a lot of things. A lot of questions is usually a good sign, provided that they aren't all hostile. An inquisitive audience signals that people were interested and paying attention, and a vibrant back-and-forth during the Q&A is exhilarating. A lack of questions is harder to gauge.

It's not true that if you explain things well you won't have any questions. Rather, your topic may not have stimulated the audience the way you had hoped. Towards the end of my own graduate career, I gave a number of presentations on far-afield (some might say pie-in-the-sky) technologies that were at least interesting to me, but I tended not to get many questions. Although the work itself was solid, the audience was not accustomed to this sort of material, and they didn't have much to say. Regardless, it's best not to fret if you don't get many questions. You should, however, make an effort to remember the questions that are asked and write them down afterwards. Or, have a fellow group member transcribe the questions as they are asked.

Returning from the Conference

After you return home from the conference, return to the checklist you put together before the conference and see how much ground you covered. Did you meet everyone you wanted to, and did you get what you wanted out of the conference? If your results fell short, it may be worth assessing if this was the appropriate conference. Use the business cards you collected to follow up on new contacts by email. Even if you only send a non-committal "it was nice to meet you" email, it is helpful to keep the lines of communication open. Also, follow up on any action items from your conversations to strengthen budding collaborations. If you promised to send someone your paper, or a link, or another document, be sure to send it. Wait a few days for that person to return home, but not more than five days or so.

A post-mortem of the conference as a whole is in order. If you presented a poster, take stock of how many visitors you had, how engaged they (and you) were about your material, and how many copies of your paper you gave away. You don't have a lot of metrics to determine how "well" you did. If you look at a conference as a means of advertising your research, then just as in the advertising industry, success may best be measured by the number of views you had, combined with how well your follow-up emails go.

If you made a full-scale presentation, now is the time to go through that list of questions you received during the Q&A. Questions, whether insightful or rudimentary, are *not* a measure of the audience's intelligence, but rather of your skill at conveying the content of your research. If questions were centered around basic material, then you may have not clearly introduced your work. The audience knows fundamental material as well as you, so if they are in fact confused, the blame most likely rests with you one way or another. And if the audience is confused about more complicated material, it is again on you to explain it clearly enough for them to get it.

It is frustrating when the audience obviously wasn't paying attention to what you said, but these failings are human nature and part of the game. You can change how you present but have little or no say over your audience. If you want to succeed and make an impression, it is necessary to alter your message until everyone understands. No one cares how singularly brilliant you are, and over-complicated explanations impress no one. If you refuse to craft your message to a comprehensible level, you will not go very far. These post-mortem insights will influence the final edits of your material. The conference may require a final version of your paper, and it is important to edit it as much as necessary based on the feedback you received.

The conference is now out of the way. Your research has been exposed to the community and critiqued, and back home in the lab you're ready to incorporate the comments into a final finished product. It's time to prepare your research for a journal article!

Chapter 8

Publishing a Journal Article

Communicating the fruits of your academic labor to the community is carried out in two ways: through conferences, which were discussed in the last chapter, and through journal articles. Conferences offer the opportunity to appear in person and meet with other researchers face-to-face, where you engage them in the ritual of networking and collaboration-building. What you achieve at the conference typically leads to a journal article. A written record of your research is published on paper (or, more commonly in this day and age, on the Internet) and archived for posterity. Journal articles almost exclusively measure the "contribution" of a grad student to his or her field and the steps to graduation.

This chapter has less to do with the quality of the research you need to communicate than with how you communicate it. A year or more of hard work, overseen by a competent advisor and nurtured by scrupulous effort on your part, likely qualifies as a contribution worthy of presentation to the community, whether at a conference, in a journal, or both. Rather, *how* you present your research is at least as important as what you're presenting. Alas, appearances really do matter at least as much as substance. Overtaxed researchers do not have the time or inclination to decipher a poorly written manuscript. Under the critical gaze of your peers, work that is incoherent, ill-composed, shoddily argued, or unsubstantiated is rooted out and torn to shreds—or worse, ignored. The most elegant results are meaningless if no one understands them, and the burden is on you to make the community take no-

tice. No matter how smart you are, the smarts must be comple-
mented by a touch of show-biz, and much success rides on your
ability to translate years of work into a crisp 7,000-word paper.

Selecting a Journal

Before your paper is even written, you should consider what journal to submit it to. It goes almost without saying that the journal must be peer-reviewed. There are a surprising number of
third-rate journals out there that tempt you with easy publication and no peer review, but papers without a review hold little or
no weight in the community. If you come across the *Egyptian Journal for Advancement of Technology* or a similar dubious-sounding
publication, run the other way, no matter what incentives they
promise. Journals of this type are exploited by dilettantes and
foreign researchers who don't have the expertise, resources, or
language skills to publish in a peer-reviewed journal. (The lack
of peer review is also a reason why conference papers carry less
weight than journal articles.)

The reputation of a journal strongly affects whether your paper is appropriate for it. Some journals publish only cutting-edge
research, whereas others are "work-horse" journals. The former
are looking for research that is hot at the moment and will make
a major impact on the field. These journals are reserved for the
big names and the big discoveries (journals like *Nature* and *Science*) and have a high "impact factor," which is important to some
people. The work-horse journals, on the other hand, are by no
means less respectable, but they are more numerous and publish
the day-to-day research that most scientists and engineers perform. They publish work that may not make as many headlines
as a *Nature* article, but they are also easier to publish in. Scoring
a high-profile publication is great, but striving for it intentionally
will most likely end in frustration. It is better to focus on producing quality work and publishing in a quality journal. Letting the
perfect be the enemy of the good may produce nothing while you
strive to conjure the next big thing to get into *Science*.

New venues for publication have emerged on the Internet that
complement the traditional journals or circumvent them entirely.
Websites like *arXiv.org* let authors announce results and post pre-

liminary papers very early, even before submission to a journal for peer review. In the competitive world of research, where first-to-discover can make or break a career, claiming a discovery up front in a respected online forum reduces the pressure of rushing a paper to a journal and prevents scooping by other researchers. When you have work that should be made available to the community as soon as possible (at least to claim credit for yourself), the Internet has resources for you. Ultimately, however, these forums are only stop-gaps on the way to publication in a journal.

If the number of journals appears overwhelming, look where your research group and colleagues have published before. Former and current authors in your group offer a wealth of information about what journals are worth dealing with and what the journals are looking for. Your advisor may insist on using particular journals. When you know the general direction to go, you have to do your own homework by reading papers the journal has already published. Perusing the titles and abstracts of a half-dozen volumes of the journal gives a clear sense of what the journal likes to publish.

What your colleagues and competition read may be the most important factor in where you choose to publish. You are publishing to be read, and to get that exposure your colleagues must have access to your work. Publication in a prestigious journal that no one in your field reads may not be as good as publishing in a run-of-the-mill journal that's popular. Your advisor and fellow group members know which journals are popular and can guide you towards the appropriate choice.

Funding is sometimes a motivating factor in journal selection, particularly in regard to page charges. Nearly all journals charge extraordinary fees for color figures (although some online publications permit free color), but some journals also charge for the black-and-white pages of every article. High-impact journals, trying to keep out the riff-raff, often have a charge just to submit an article for consideration. The suitability of a journal and the fees that come with it depend on your funding. In an unfunded research group as a graduate student, I was restricted to the half-dozen journals that were relevant to my field and didn't charge to publish accepted papers (in black and white, that is). If you have plenty of research funding, this won't be an issue. Most likely, your PI handles the money and will let you know how many color figures he's willing to pay for.

Conforming to Journal Guidelines

Preparing your journal article involves much more than worrying about *what* you are going to write. *How* you write it is important, and doing your homework ahead of time will save a lot of headaches. Many researchers write their manuscripts without knowing where they intend to submit the article, and so they write it in the format that they prefer. Unfortunately, each journal has a different format, and as a money-making (or at least break-even) venture, the journal does not have the resources to vary from that format or do the formatting for you.

By choosing the submission journal ahead of time, you have the chance to visit the journal's website and read up on its formatting guidelines. Each journal has its own look and feel. These defining characteristics are described in a document that you can find somewhere on the journal's website, and they must be followed to the letter. The guidelines govern every detail of your paper except for the content. They specify the number of words allowed in a figure caption, how to abbreviate equations, the number of lines in a table, font size in figures, accepted spelling of certain words (e.g., "center" vs. "centre"), and prohibited usage of other words (for example, not using "while" in place of "whereas"). Abiding by these rules is necessary for your paper to be considered by the journal, and not following them could get your paper rejected at the very start. I have seen submissions rejected for so much as missing periods in figure captions or for inappropriate use of boldface. Usually these rejections have nothing to do with the content, and once you play by the journal's rules, you can resubmit and move on to the review process.

Journal format standards include fonts and font size, column width, page margins, figure placement, page size, and many more. Conforming to those requirements would be difficult on your own, so most journals offer a template online. The template usually comes in Microsoft Word and LaTeX formats and is predesigned with the journal's structure in place, including example figures and captions, equations, tables, reference lists, and other important elements. It is your job to replace the stand-in material with your own, while taking care to follow the other guidelines that the template can't take into account for you, like word usage and equation length. By choosing your journal ahead of time, you have the chance to download this template and write your paper from scratch according to the journal's guidelines. If you don't, you may spend many hours converting your paper to something the journal will accept.

On occasion, you will encounter a journal that does not publish explicit formatting guidelines. Even without a document of rules and regulations, you don't have carte blanche to compose anything you like and submit it. The journal's style should become clear after reading a few papers. The journal may offer more leeway with minor aspects of manuscript formatting, such as the length of figure captions, but an overall style remains, and you should aim for this equilibrium in your writing.

Writing Your Paper

This chapter isn't about how to write a technical paper. Like other topics in grad school, whole books are available on technical writing. Instead, a few general comments are in order. As you compose your manuscript, the journal's needs must be kept in mind. Above all, there is a premium on space. Editors squeeze every last column-inch out of accepted articles, and you can generate good will by being concise from the very start. Vertical space is most precious and most often taken up by equations. Although the journal guidelines often do not discuss equation size, equations that are kept short and horizontal (for example, using "/" for fractions instead of a full-size numerator and denominator) are most desirable. This is another area where planning ahead saves you from having to go back and edit all of your equations.

The journal also has different expectations depending on the type of article you submit: a full paper, a technical note, or a survey paper. Full papers are the most common and are what you need to graduate, as they constitute the contribution of new and original research to your field. A technical note (sometimes called a "letter") is shorter, sometimes much shorter (perhaps only a page or two), and covers a narrow topic. A note or letter is published more quickly than a full article, and therefore they may include a time-sensitive discovery. A note is either an early report on such a discovery (often followed up with a fleshed-out article) or on entirely too narrow a subject to warrant a full article.

A survey paper is very long, twice as long as a full paper, and provides a broad discussion of a research topic by referencing a hundred or more journal articles and putting them together into a narrative on the trends of research. Survey articles are most commonly composed by well established researchers in the field and by invitation of the journal.

These different forms of publications play different roles on your resume and on your path to graduation, and their relative impact varies widely from field to field and journal to journal. In some fields (such as aerospace engineering), technical notes and letters, while useful for the community, are published quickly with a minimum of peer review and therefore don't "count." On the other hand, in the prestigious journal *Nature*, nearly all papers are three-page "letters" and constitute major scientific contributions. Full-scale articles in any journal are thoroughly peer-reviewed reports of original research and carry great weight. With experience, you will identify the balance of importance among notes, letters, and articles in your field. Survey articles contain no original research and probably count the least on your resume, although—from the perspective of preparing you for research—they may be the most useful.

Brevity is the soul of publishing. If you're writing a new paper from scratch, make your points as quickly as possible and spare the reader excessive verbiage. An old conference paper provides an opportunity to edit down, rather than build up. Conference papers typically contain a lot of detail and technical material, which is helpful for documenting the work you have done, but it does not contribute much to the research question at hand. If you're converting a conference paper to a journal article, you have to cut out that extraneous material.

You have no doubt composed many reports before, and although I hesitate to write about the construction of a journal article, I will nonetheless hazard a few words about the various parts that constitute your upcoming publication:

- **Abstract.** Most subscribers to a journal will read nothing more than this 200-word blurb that you compose mostly as an afterthought. After writing the bulk of the paper over several months in a perpetually sleep-deprived state, the abstract looms over you as another tedious exercise that seems to merit as little effort as possible. However, given that most of your colleagues will only read the abstract, it is arguably the place where you should spend the *most* effort, and make it as striking and memorable as possible. The abstract is your journal article in miniature. A sentence of historical context, a sentence about your objective or hypothesis, a sentence or two for your experiments, and another for your results. You have to explain to the reader in a few words why your results are amazing and why he or she should read the whole article. If a casual browser of the journal can read your abstract and walk away knowing what you did, why you did it, and why anyone should care, you've written a quality abstract. Don't be afraid to include detail; numbers often speak louder than words. If a peer in your field is reading your abstract, an ambiguous description that you found "several fast trajectories to Mars" won't have nearly the same eyebrow-raising power as announcing that you found "a 10-day trajectory to Mars that repeats every 20 days."

- **Introduction.** The article you're writing may be a new contribution to the field, but you didn't get here on your own. Hundreds of years of history, thousands of past researchers, and millions of experiments underpin the results that you want to publish, and the introduction section is where posterity gets its credit. No scientist works in a vacuum, and you must provide the context that motivates your research. What field exactly are you working in? Who are the players? What have they found thus far? What gap in current knowledge urged you to bother with this paper? The introduction is where ten, twenty, thirty journal articles are referenced to place your work in historical context. Reviewers like to see that you have assigned the appropriate credit (even better when the work of the reviewers themselves is referenced), and future grad students will use this meticulously recorded history when it's their turn to follow in your footsteps. The introduction is where you finally reveal to the reader what you're trying to do: state your hypothesis or objective, and explain what impact the possible results will have on that historical context. The introduction is *not* a place to draft a textbook. It is tempting to fill pages with math and other calculations that took so long to learn, but you must suppress that urge. If background material can be off-loaded to a reference, it should be. A journal article is not a forum to lecture your peers.

- **Experiments and Methodology.** In some fields, "experiment" and "methodology" are synonymous. In others, the "methodology" defines the philosophy behind a particular battery of experiments; that is, the choice of methodology influences which experiments are chosen to test a hypothesis. Depending on your field, you may use one, both, or neither in your journal articles. Theorists, for example, may not perform "experiments" per se, and instead substitute a section on "numerical methods." Whichever way your field approaches its problems, at some point you have to describe what you *did*, and that information goes here. What equipment did you use? What settings? How long did the experiments run and under what conditions? What step size did you use in your numerical integrator? Did you assume a horse was a sphere to make the calculations more tractable? Above all, why did you make these choices (the methodology)? After reading this section of your paper, a reader should have all the information he or she needs to reproduce everything you did.

- **Results.** After you've run your experiments, the results section displays your data in all its glory, condensed to the metrics and measurements that make the point you set out in your introduction. Many papers mix the results and experiments sections—if, for example, the results of one experiment affect the execution of others. It should be clear to the reader what results correspond to what experiments, the units you've used, and, if your quoted results are derived from other calculations, how you calculated them. Once again, the goal is to clarify how to reproduce your experiments, and other researchers must know exactly what results to expect from each experiment.

- **Discussion.** Authors go to great lengths in the discussion section to address how their experiments and results did exactly what they wanted them to do. Do the results conform with expectations, or were there some surprises? Do you reject your null hypothesis? Do the results show that you successfully synthesized the desired compound? Less frequently do authors use the discussion section for its other purpose: self-critique. When you submit your article to a journal, peers in your field will review every sentence looking for holes in your story, and the discussion section is your opportunity to head some of them off. Your methodology may explain why you performed particular experiments and how they prove your point, but what if you had followed a different methodology? What if you had made slightly different assumptions? What if the horse wasn't a sphere, but a cube instead? What if you changed the step size in your integrator? How could these changes affect the results, and is there a reasonable expectation that your conclusions could be different because of them? Be forthcoming about the assumptions and the shortcomings of your methods. The discussion section isn't trying to prove your results wrong, but it does signal to the community that you have not planned your experiments in a vacuum, that you are aware of the domain in which your results are valid, and that your conclusions still hold up under such scrutiny.

- **Conclusion.** The conclusion is the most abused section of papers published today. After warning readers in the abstract what the paper is going to tell them, and after boring them with a dry recitation of experiments and results in the body text, most authors treat the conclusion—the authors' one moment to sum up this work that supposedly merits a publication—as an opportunity to simply repeat the content of the abstract. The readers learn yet again about what experiments were run, what methodologies were followed, and what the outcomes were: the very things they just read! It is painfully rare to see a conclusion that actually *concludes* anything. A "conclusion" section is not meant just to end an article; the conclusion puts your results into context. Any researcher can write about how his or her results show a "statistically significant signal consistent with the Higgs boson," but the conclusion should also mention that this result confirms 50 years of theory in elementary particle physics. The results were the signal: the measurement, the description of a new fossil, the validation or refutation of a null hypothesis. The *conclusion* tells the readers what that result *means*. The conclusion section should answer a simple question: "So what?" By the end of the article, what do we know now that we didn't know before, and why should anyone care? If you don't answer this question now in your written publications, you *will* in a couple years at your defense.

Overall, watch your spelling and grammar. For all the hurdles raised during the peer review process, there never seems to be anyone ultimately responsible for (or interested in) tidying up your writing style. Misspelled words and wonky grammar sneak their way through peers, associate editors, and copy editors and appear in unforgiving print forever. You want your readers (and especially your reviewers) to be happy. Poor wordsmithing is irritating, either by forcing them to put the article down in frustration or, in the case of the reviewer, by causing them to turn a more critical eye than they might have otherwise.

It is also wise to be generous with your references. No doubt you hope that your paper will make waves in the field and be referenced for decades to come. Your peers feel the same way about their papers, and it is polite to oblige where appropriate. Young researchers tend to put in a minimum of references, partially because they haven't yet seen all the literature that's out there, and also because they like to think of their work standing on its own merit more than it really does. Rarely can you include too many references. You always want to reference the most original related work (that is, going back to the oldest applicable reference, rather than the most convenient one you have on your desk), but also referencing contemporary work, which places your research in context and makes it clear that you're cognizant of the latest goings-on in the field.

The order of authors on your paper is another delicate issue that should be resolved as quickly and painlessly as possible. A lot of ego is associated with where names appear on the author list, and a fine balance of politics and tradition contributes to the sequence of names that appears on your paper. Usually the person who leads the research and who literally writes the paper appears first. Presumably this is you. After doing all the research, presenting it at a conference, and typing up the results, you are unequivocally the "author." However, some research groups have different rules for precedence, for example putting the driving intellectual force of the research first. If you're a young graduate student, and the PI was the one who conceived the research problem and shepherded much of the research itself, the PI may be the one who prefers to be first author (and there's not much arguing against a PI). In the case that the results of your research are especially controversial, the PI may want his or her name first to take the heat off you. An established name in the field can afford to make bolder claims and be noticed for them, whereas an inexperienced student may end up ignored if your results rock the boat. If this isn't the case, the trend these days is for your advisor or the PI to appear *last*, and there has been just as much jockeying among researchers for the last position on the author list as for the first. For papers with lots of authors (some large collaborations publish with two or three dozen authors), the list is frequently alphabetical after the first few names of the major contributors.

Submitting Your Manuscript

Journal submissions today are done almost exclusively on the Internet. At the journal's website, you create a profile and are asked to submit an electronic version of your manuscript. Very few journals accept paper submissions of any kind. You are assigned an associate editor, who is your point of contact at the journal. This person manages your submission on the journal's end, herds the peer reviewers and keeps them on task, and makes the decision on acceptance of your paper to the journal.

The next controversial challenge is suggesting reviewers for your article. Not all journals request these suggestions, but many do to save themselves time from searching out appropriate peer reviewers. You can consult your advisor for ideas, but there are some rules of thumb. It is best that you know whom you are nominating as a reviewer. If there are people you know who are critical specifically of your work or subject area, it is not wise to nominate them. A critical eye improves your paper, but you don't want to butt heads. Nominate people whom you expect to offer constructive criticism without unnecessary conflict.

Famous people make for bad suggested reviewers. They are too busy to be bothered with you, a lowly grad student, and will probably turn down the review request anyway. Plus, getting turned down by a potential reviewer makes your associate editor's job harder, something you don't want to happen. Worse, if a famous person does accept a review request, there's no telling what they might say! And although reviews are supposed to be anonymous, nothing stops the reviewers from signing their comments, and you'll be in a very poor position to contradict a comment from a famous researcher. Similarly, don't suggest anyone who is already an editor or associate editor. They are also too busy, and reviewing your paper could be a conflict interest.

If you can't make a quick list off the top of your head, make nominations based on your paper's list of references. If you do nominate from the reference list, make sure that the suggested reviewers are, in fact, alive. I once nearly suggested two dead researchers to an editor before my advisor stepped in and corrected me.

After you select a list of reviewers to nominate (three to five names), go back to your manuscript and see if you reference these people's articles. If they are expert enough to review your technical work, most likely they have contributed to the field in some way that is relevant to your paper, and that warrants a reference. Also, it is common courtesy. People like seeing themselves referenced. It may not be the way a perfect world would work, but in the real world this kind of bribery doesn't hurt. If you don't reference them and they end up being a reviewer, don't be surprised if the "anonymous" reviewer suggests adding references that suspiciously have all the same author.

Ultimately, the associate editor may not use any of your suggested reviewers, which is his or her prerogative. Since the reviewers remain anonymous, you may never know if the editor takes your suggestions or not. If the journal does not give you the option to nominate reviewers, the editor will probably take names from your reference list.

Once you submit the manuscript, your fate is in the hands of the journal and the associate editor, who passes the document to your peers for review. And now you wait. And wait. And wait.

The Peer Reviewer

For your first journal article, the role of the peer reviewer is mysterious. Months go by without hearing anything from the journal, and then early one morning you awake to find an email in your inbox with page after page of commentary that seems to make all your work for naught. You will expend plenty of energy cursing the reviewer for complicating your life. But before that review comes back, let us examine what the reviewer's job is and, equally importantly, what it's not.

The reviewer is the only line of defense between your article and an archived eternity in the annals of research, and it is his or her responsibility to ensure both that your work has value to the community and that the article merits publication in this particular journal. The metrics with which the reviewer evaluates your paper are unique to each reviewer. Some may subjectively weigh your work and see if it passes the "smell test." Others roll up their sleeves and check every line of your math. Others pull out a stack of journals and check the validity of your references. Reviewers examine the precision of numerical computations for theoretical work, and they place the statistical results of empirical research under the metaphorical microscope. They assess whether your methodology and techniques are up to date and whether they are likely to yield the results you claim. The reviewer checks for completeness and ensures that your paper includes all of the material they expect (e.g., does your introduction actually introduce the topic, or just re-hash textbook material? Does your discussion section cast the properly critical eye on your own work?). The reviewer judges whether your conclusions are in fact supported by the results of your experiments; if not, should more experiments be recommended, or is there something fundamentally flawed with the hypothesis? Good reviewers include a balance of all these functions.

The peer reviewer has the strongest voice deciding whether your work constitutes a contribution to your field. Every day, journals receive submissions that describe interesting work but don't merit publication, either because the advance of knowledge is too small or the results are too trivial. Textbooks are full of homework problems whose solutions have never been published in a journal and never will be, because no one who reads the journal would benefit by their publication. Calculating pi to one digit more than the previous grad student barely qualifies as something new to the field. A scholarly journal is not a repository of facts or a book of world records.

A peer reviewer is concerned with archiving an advancement in our understanding of the world and the methods by which the world is understood. The trillionth-and-first digit of pi may not merit publication, but the groundbreaking method you used to find that last digit probably would. Where the line is drawn is subjective and interpreted differently by each reviewer. Under the guidance of your advisor and your own hard-won experience, you will gradually come to understand how far your efforts must extend to ensure that you're on the right side of that line.

With so much responsibility resting on the reviewer's shoulders, there are some tasks that he or she will not oblige you with. The reviewer is not expected to (and usually won't) check formatting, grammar, and spelling. It is your job to prepare a quality final draft, and the reviewer will not rewrite material for you. These checks, if they belong to anyone, belong to the associate editor, or, later, to the copy editor. If your writing is exceptionally sloppy, the reviewer or editor may return the manuscript to you unreviewed and demand a rewrite before proceeding. Thorough proof-reading before submission is key to making the reviewer's job as painless as possible. A reviewer irritated by shoddy word-smithing is that much more likely to be extra critical of the rest of your paper. Some reviewers kindly help with grammatical foibles and slips of style, but that help may not be so welcome when the reviewer's commentary goes on for sixty bullet points about comma placements and your choice of prepositions (I've been on the giving *and* receiving ends of that!).

The reviewer is also not expected to design your research for you. Many researchers unfortunately submit preliminary results or experiments that are at a dead end, hoping that the reviewer will make helpful suggestions to reignite the author's research. No reviewer has the time to coddle your research in addition to carrying out their own. A journal article should describe a complete story, from hypothesis to conclusions, without the need for

an overhaul by an outside observer. The reviewer is there to review your work, not become a co-author. A half-finished journal
article rarely begets the assistance from reviewers that the author
wants, and instead usually leads to instant rejection and the ever-
lasting enmity of both editor and reviewers.

The reviewer is busy, and probably doesn't want to do the
review at all. Once you enter the work force, for every paper
that you publish, you can be expected to review three articles in
penance, and the more prominent in the field you become, the
more popular you become as a reviewer. The reviewer still agrees
to these review requests, both to stay in the good graces of the
journal and because, ultimately, the ongoing health of the field
depends on active participation in the publication process.

Even though it is part of their job description, the reviewer
will probably not go through any gritty details. It took months of
research to work out all your math, so you can't imagine the reviewer is interested in comprehending and critiquing it in only
a few hours. For this reason, you cannot expect the reviewer
to double-check anything in your equations. The reviewer isn't
there to be your editor or to subsidize laziness. If you are sloppy
with your documentation, that sloppiness will probably make it
through the entire publication process uncorrected. A few typos
are bound to appear somewhere in your final manuscript no matter how careful you are, especially if you have lots of mathematics,
but the reviewers really cannot be blamed for these oversights.

The reviewer's job sounds intimidating, but keep in mind that
reviewers have a vested interest in seeing your work published.
No one has anything to gain if rejection were commonplace. In
a dystopian system riddled with rejection notices and impossibly
high bars to publication, research would grind to a halt and the
reviewers themselves wouldn't be able to get published. Furthermore, reviewers that have been referenced in your own manuscript
are keen to see your paper in print, as references are a major factor in career visibility. The reviewer ensures that standards are
maintained, but also that the flow of publication continues.

If you have a busy advisor, you might end up with the job of
reviewer yourself. After doing reviews for a decade or two, the
privilege loses its luster and the temptation is great to pawn off
the job to underlings, who are already bound to do his bidding
and who would probably benefit from the experience. Your advi-

sor may hand you the task *sub rosa*, in which case nobody knows
that you actually did the review, or he may forward your name
to the journal for the review, often with an assurance that he will
"supervise" your review. Either way, while undertaking this hal-
lowed task, it is important to remember the Golden Rule: do unto
other authors as you would have them do unto you!

Return of the Review

When the review of your paper finally arrives, it will have been
been quite a while. The review usually takes a few months, but
sometimes it takes more than a year! This amount of time depends entirely on the journal and how fervidly the journal en-
forces deadlines on reviewers. Almost no one working for a journal gets paid, and there may not be much motivation to move the
papers along. Journals have restricted funding, which slows the
publication process. If it's looking like the journal won't be able
to afford printing thick editions this year, the editor-in-chief and
other powers-that-be may instruct editors to rein in the rate of
manuscript reviews and stem the tide.

The review itself is a document or email from the associate
editor that lists the comments of the reviewers. The reviewers
themselves never contact you directly. The review is usually a
numbered or bulleted list of comments on particular issues, frequently with a preamble in which the reviewer describes his or her
overall take on the paper. Sometimes you receive a scanned document of your manuscript with hand-written comments by the
reviewer, which is common when the reviewer wishes to suggest
edits that are hard to describe in words, such as moving blocks
of text around. The review also contains comments from the associate editor him or herself, including stylistic and formatting
corrections, which are necessary to stay in line with the journal's
standards, and comments on the content as the editor sees fit to
make. The editors are themselves professionals in your field and
are more than capable of critiquing your work. The associate editor may also request wording changes for political reasons. The
journal has a reputation to maintain and a business to run, and it
may not be comfortable printing inflammatory material, such as
disparaging arguments against other researchers or veiled sniping

at funding agencies.

There are always two or more reviews of your manuscript, performed anonymously.* Each review is as unique as the person writing it. You may receive two long reviews, or one short and one long. You may get bulleted lists of comments, or you may get blocks of prose. Some reviewers, being short on time, provide little more than a summary and faint praise in a paragraph and offer no constructive advice, whereas others pontificate for pages and pages. Seldom will the editor let all the reviews be short and unconstructive. If you end up with multiple reviewers doing a thorough job of it, you'll find that many comments overlap and that things aren't as bad as they look.

First and foremost: don't take the comments personally! The reviewers probably don't know you, although they may recognize your advisor's name. As you go through the pages of commentary, don't panic. Being asked to revise your work is a good thing! If you've received a review (as opposed to a rejection, which is discussed at the end of this chapter), it means your paper will probably be published after all, once you've gone through the hoops of heeding the reviewers' comments. Also, the review itself is a sign that your peers recognize the merit of your efforts. With additional edits from the community, the reviewers believe your work can be archived for posterity. The comments are meant to be constructive. Once you have incorporated them into your manuscript, your paper *will* be stronger.

Despite the lofty goals of reviewing a journal manuscript, the process has an ugly side as well. Your review is guaranteed to have some downright stupid comments in it: the kind of comments that make you tear your hair out and wonder whether the reviewer even read your paper at all; the kind of comments that are so frivolous you wonder if you have to address them; the kind of comments that are so poorly worded that you don't actually know what the reviewer is asking you to change.

Reviewers are people, too. They have their own quirks and biases, just like your own quirky advisor. They may have an ir-

_____

*For some reviewers, ego trumps the power of anonymity. On occasion, a reviewer suggests further experimentation or analysis that they feel holds great promise. On the off chance that the suggestion bears fruit, I have seen a reviewer sign his review and explicitly ask for credit in the updated manuscript if the results are interesting!

rational (to you!) preference for certain methods that they subsequently insist on, or they may prefer that you reference previous work in a particular way. There will be nitpicking of things that you think are irrelevant. Reviewers have asked me to change the wording of one phrase that I think is perfectly clear to something the reviewer prefers but is more ambiguous. I have been asked to change the order of items in tables and lists. I regularly receive comments about the thickness of lines in a plot or about the font size in a figure.

Off-topic comments are common. Some reviewers have peculiar bugaboos and insist that you comment on a tangential issue that has little to do with your paper. They may suggest that you investigate an unrelated side issue that interests them. Reviewers live in their own research world in the same way you do, and what you consider tangential, they consider essential. As you edit your manuscript and prepare a response to the comments, you must strike a balance between staying on topic and satisfying the reviewer.

Misinformed comments are the easiest to deal with but are the most frustrating. The reviewer may ask questions that were answered elsewhere in the paper, or it may become clear that the reviewer did not read the paper very carefully. It is frustrating to wait so long for a review only to discover that the paper wasn't given its due. These comments can be dealt with mostly by pointing out that they were already addressed. However, keep in mind that *most people in the community will read your paper just as superficially as this reviewer*, and if you weren't clear for him or her, you may want to add in a redundant explanation and save future readers their own frustration.

It is possible that your review will be performed by colleagues in a competing research group. Depending on your relationship with that group, the comments may be unfair or petty, or they may recommend demoting your submission from a full journal article to a technical letter. In the modern battle for research dollars, it may benefit your competition to be especially harsh and look for ways to hamper your own progress, so that you'll have a harder time acquiring resources that they can then poach. This scenario is uncommon, but by no means unheard of, and you should keep in mind that you may face it. The associate editor's role is to play referee in situations like this and to make sure that the review process is fair.

Updating Your Manuscript

The purpose of the review is to improve your manuscript, and as you go through these comments you must update the text accordingly. In addition to editing the manuscript itself, you are expected to provide the associate editor with a response to the review (sometimes called a "rebuttal"), in which you outline explicitly how you have addressed the reviewers' comments. Without this extra document, the editor has no way of knowing what you've done to respond to the review.

Most importantly, never quibble with the reviewer's comment! The associate editor does not know you and may not be qualified to understand your work in detail, so he only has the reviewer comments to determine the merit of your paper. The reviewer has the undisputed final word. Each reviewer comment must be addressed item by item. You cannot pick and choose which comments you feel are most appropriate. Even if comments overlap among reviewers, be prepared to address each one in your article and in the response document.

Every reviewer comment should correspond to an edit of some kind in the paper, no matter how trivial. Reviewers frequently ask rhetorical questions of the authors without reference to a particular part of the document. The reviewer may never see your response, and the associate editor doesn't care what the answer is, so you need to find a spot somewhere—anywhere—that you can incorporate a response to the reviewer's mental meanderings. A single off-hand sentence in the middle of the text, for example, often suffices.

Nitpicky comments must be addressed, no matter how irritating. You can surely find one turn of phrase or another to accommodate the reviewer's stylistic and grammatical peccadilloes. A reviewer of mine once insisted that the word "so" can't be used as a coordinating conjunction (as in the sentence "I was hungry, so I ate lunch") and that my manuscript should be sanitized of the incriminating particle. The MLA Style Guide and I respectfully disagreed, but it was easier to simply change the half-dozen instances of the word in my manuscript than to start a battle that would drag an unhappy editor in to mediate.

In the rare case that a comment is undoubtedly the product of a lax review or of the reviewer being plainly mistaken, an edit may not be necessary. However, such instances must be kept to a minimum, no matter how bad the review you are dealing with. In a review with 30–40 comments, I would ration no more than two opportunities to outright disregard a comment.

Sometimes you can have fun with trivial comments. During one review process, I encountered a reviewer who insisted on principle that references should go as far back as possible to the original source. I heartily agree in principle, but the reviewer in this case was referring to my use of a fundamental equation from introductory physics, and including a reference to this equation was as silly as referencing Pythagoras for finding a hypotenuse. However, being loathe to dismiss a reviewer comment, I began a literature search, and after some effort, I uncovered the original paper from 1865 that introduced the law for the first time. My journal article ended up with a 150-year-old reference tucked in among the modern scholarship. I am sure the reviewer and the editor were satisfied.

In addition to the edited manuscript, you submit the response detailing how you addressed the reviewers' comments. To make the associate editor's life as easy as possible, it is best to respond to each comment point by point, using the same numbering or bulleting scheme of each reviewer. Before getting into the meat of your response, be sure to include a paragraph at the beginning thanking the reviewers and the editor for their time.

Your response (or "rebuttal") document should always be professional. Even if the reviewers have sent you on wild goose chases and burdened you with a mountain of grammatical corrections, you should remain above the fray. Snarky, condescending, dismissive, or defensive responses get you nowhere. A cool and respectful deference to each comment keeps the editor from having to play arbiter. Even if the editor would secretly agree with you that a comment is frivolous, it is better for him to remain impartial. You shouldn't be drawn into an argument by a combative reviewer. A painless edit by you makes the problem go away and saves your editor a lot of frustration. Remember, the journal doesn't have to publish your article, and the editor is the sole gatekeeper.

Each item in your response has several components. First, there must be an explicit description of how the comment was addressed. This can include an explanation of your motivation, but the response document is not a place to lecture. The response should not have the tone of addressing either the reviewers or the editor. Do not answer the reviewers' questions in the response itself. Those questions should be answered by a change in the updated manuscript.

For every change in the text, the response should have a reference to the page, paragraph, and line number in the paper where the edit was made and it should contain a complete quote of the new or edited text, no matter how long. The associate editor is not nearly as familiar with your paper as you are, and he is not inclined to compare the old and new copies. It costs nothing to include the full text of your changes. When a reviewer once asked me to rewrite my abstract and conclusion sections, I added three pages of quoted text to my response, for which I am sure the editor was eternally thankful.

As several months pass between the submission of your article and the return of the review, it is possible that you will have found errors or decided on improvements that the reviewers themselves didn't pick up on. You can change your manuscript however you like, even beyond what the reviewers request, but be warned that if your unsolicited changes contain technical content, the editor may send the paper back to the reviewers.

Submit the Updated Manuscript

When your edits and the response are done, you submit them to the associate editor in the same way you submitted the original manuscript. Now you wait some more.

There is a good chance that the editor will send your revised manuscript back to the reviewers. The process is the same as the first time, although the comments that come back are substantially fewer. You should respond to the new comments in the same fashion as before. Depending on the mood of the reviewers and the editor, you may go through several cycles. No matter how exasperating, you have to roll with the punches. If the editor doesn't return the article to the reviewers, he may still have some

Submission Process

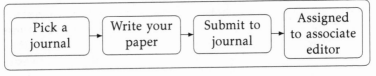

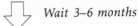 *Wait 3–6 months*

Review Cycle

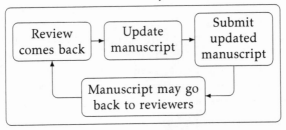

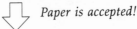 *Paper is accepted!*

Copy-Editing Process

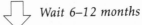 *Wait 6–12 months*

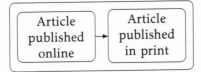

The Publication Process

last comments of his own for you to address.

Once the associate editor is satisfied with your edits, the paper is accepted. Congratulations!

But the paperwork is not yet over. At this stage you are asked about copyright. You should consult with your advisor on this tricky legal issue. Most journals prefer to have the copyright of your article transferred over to them, but that is not always necessary. If you don't have to transfer the copyright, *don't*. If you give up your copyright, you give up the right to distribute your own paper or to post it online. If you can, retain the copyright for yourself and for all your co-authors.

Some journals make copyright transfer a requirement of publication. In that case, the journal usually includes a clause in the agreement that allows you and the co-authors to distribute the paper yourself and on your own website. When it comes to accepting this situation or not getting published at all, it's best to go with what the journal wants. You'll gain far more from getting your article in print than being a stickler about copyright retention.

After your acceptance comes in, you are introduced to yet another kind of editor: the copy editor. This individual is responsible for transforming the document that you submitted into something that can be printed in the journal. The copy editor checks the fine details, such as font sizes, the resolution of figures, and the formatting of your references. He or she also checks that the references correspond to real documents.

During the review process the only document the reviewers and editors saw was a finished and compiled manuscript. In the final publication phase, you send in raw text and image files. The copy editor toys with these files and creates a new document, called the "page proof" (or, formerly, "galley proof"), that conforms to the style of the journal. This proof most likely looks completely different from the document you compiled yourself, and you have no say over how the copy editor has organized your figures and tables. The journal-ready article will use multiple columns and single spacing, will shift figures around accounting for aesthetics, and will alter equations to fit properly on the page.

After the copy editor is finished, you receive the proof and yet another mini-review with it, in which the editor asks questions about formatting and wording and asks for your approval of the proofs. At this point, there is no more editing allowed beyond the issues the copy editor has brought up. You cannot make any changes to the technical content, but you are still well advised to go through the proof with a fine-toothed comb. The editor will have specific questions for you, but other formatting changes may have been made without comment. In some cases those changes may be incorrect, and you should bring those problems up. For example, in a paper I once wrote, an overzealous copy editor replaced a few instances of the number "7" with the word "seven," even though the original number was a numerical result that should have remained a numeral. The copy editor did not announce these changes to me, and only a careful review of the page proof revealed the editor's error.

Once you approve the page proof, it's off to the presses! After a few weeks or months, the journal informs you of your publication date. The online publication may be immediate, but the printed version is typically several months to a year in the future.

Rejection

Before ending this chapter, I want to address the possibility that your paper is rejected. The best way to avoid a rejection is to make sure that your advisor knows what's going on with your research and that he approves your own plans for publication, namely that he has read your manuscript and approves of the journal you have selected. I have had the misfortune as a reviewer of recommending rejection of papers that, by their poor composition and sloppy documentation, had clearly never been read by the student's advisor, who was listed as the second author.

There are a number of reasons why your paper may be rejected, and the associate editor will explain them to you. Sometimes it is the reviewers who recommend rejection, and sometimes the editor makes the decision separately. The latter case occurs, for example, if you have chosen an inappropriate journal and the editor believes your paper does not fit into the scope of the publication. Your paper may not have enough impact for the journal to publish. The journal *Nature* is in the business of publishing groundbreaking work that receives a lot of attention, not run-of-the-mill research articles.

The reviewers may reject your paper based on uncertainty in the originality of your work. If that's the case, then your advisor isn't doing his job! You should reevaluate your research plan with your advisor and make sure that the work you are doing can ultimately lead to those precious publications. As a reviewer I once recommended rejection of a paper that spent 30 pages pontificating on fundamental material (which could have been off-loaded to a reference or two) before getting to a very thin 2 pages of new research. That author's advisor should have stepped in much earlier in the writing process and prevented the submission from happening in the first place.

Poor wordsmithing is another common reason for rejection. It is wise to constantly evaluate your writing skills and have peers read your manuscripts before sending them off for review. Unfortunately, many science and engineering programs emphasize technical curriculum at the expense of broader skills in the humanities, and new graduate students coming out of these programs find it challenging to eloquently and effectively communicate their research. If English is not your native language, the burden is even greater to ensure that your manuscript maintains an acceptable (and coherent) standard.

If you receive a rejection, there are a few possible steps to take in the future. You could submit your paper to a more appropriate journal if it was rejected on grounds of scope or impact. You must take care, however, which alternative journals you choose. The associate editor may directly suggest a sibling journal from the same society that publishes more appropriate content.

For wordsmithing rejections, your best hope is to work with several willing peers to bring your writing up to snuff, and with native English speakers if language is a problem. (Having a native speaker of English review your paper for improvements is a wise move regardless of whether your paper was rejected or not.) For other content-related rejections, you should consult with your advisor. You and he will evaluate the options moving forward, whether revamping the paper to address the source of the rejection, or even dropping the paper entirely.

By producing a few quality papers, the highest hurdle towards graduation is surmounted. Although the process from the first written words to glossy print can take one or two years, the satisfaction of holding a thick, bound journal in your hands with your name on it is infinitely satisfying. No matter what happens to you or your research afterwards, that journal article is archived forever. One, ten, or a hundred years from now, an over-caffeinated and underpaid grad student like you just might stumble upon your article, and the reference you get—your contribution, at long last—is worth all the effort.

Chapter 9

The Bureaucracy

It was my first day of grad school. I was new to the university, had just moved into town, and had a list of errands burning a hole in my pocket: register for classes, apply for financial aid, get a parking permit, get through orientation. But before anyone can do anything at a university, you must have your ID card, and I had queued up in the campus union to get mine. After waiting in a line that stretched down the hall and around the corner, my turn finally came. I stepped up to the woman at the front desk and declared my request for an ID. She replied, "What's your student ID number?" My ID number? How am I supposed to know? I just got here. "Well, it should be on your card." But I don't have an ID card. That's why I'm here. Can't you use my name? "Even with your name, we still need the ID number to make the card." You can't look it up? "No. We can't. You have to look it up yourself. You can log into one of the computers around the corner."

Around the corner were a pair of aging desktop computers. I abandoned my place in line, woke up a computer, and was greeted by a window asking for a user name and password. But I don't know my user name and password, because I'm not in the system yet. I can't log in. The woman back at the desk tells me to go down to the basement, where I will find an office for computer help.

There is another line in the basement, where I wait for someone who can help me. When I reach the front of the line, I explain that I'm a new grad student and that I don't know my user name or password for logging into the campus computers. "Do you have your ID card?" Ugh. No. I don't have it yet. I'm new. "Well, do you know your number?" I'm down here so I can log in to get the number! The folks upstairs said I needed to log in to get the number. "Huh. That shouldn't be necessary. What's your name?" I give him my name. He types, and types some more. "Well, I can't find your account on the network." Ugh! "Have you not registered for classes?" How could I? I just moved here yesterday. "You need to have registered for classes to get added to our system." So to get my ID card, I need my ID number, but to get that number I need to log into the campus network. But I can't log into the network unless I've registered for classes, which I can't do unless I have my card and ID number?*

The Emergent Phenomenon

If you need to register for classes, apply for financial aid, get reimbursed for travel, get forms signed for graduation, or submit a thesis, you must grapple with the monster of academic bureaucracy. You must submit to policies, practices, rules, and regulations that may not make sense, may be contradictory, and whose administrators only execute—rather than understand—the rules they enforce. Getting through grad school means getting through the bureaucracy. The university has erected many roadblocks between you and graduation, and getting through those roadblocks has nothing to do with skill, talent, or intelligence. Instead, you must diligently fill out your documents in triplicate, submit them to the properly designated authorities, and wait patiently for paper to be moved the requisite number of times.

   Bureaucracy is an emergent phenomenon of human organization. When enough people come together with a common purpose (say, running a university), the system inevitably slows under its own weight and a bureaucracy takes over. Examples of bureaucracy go back to the beginnings of human civilization: the Roman Empire, the Persian Empire, and the ancient Egyptians all had extensive bureaucracies to manage vast territories; the Tang, Song, Ming, and Qing dynasties in China implemented rigorous examinations that determined who would be allowed to serve in the imperial bureaucracy. Today we are surrounded by bureaucracies

---

*This is a true story. The university's system has improved marginally since.

at our places of work, places of learning, places of worship, and government. Bureaucracy is a side-effect of human interaction, and anyone who tries to devise a system that won't develop a bureaucracy is doomed to failure. The only choice for those of us who must interact with the bureaucracy is to understand what it is, who is in it, and how to manipulate it to our advantage.

Small organizations, like the corner coffee shop or a church bake sale, can manage themselves with a minimum of internal or external interference. The man or woman in charge of the group handles the necessary paperwork, or each worker pitches in to keep the system running smoothly. This is the ideal that we wish would last forever. Financial investors reminisce about sprightly young companies that could react to competition instantly and keep revenues growing. We remember the old days when the church choir only had eight people and could sing whatever it wanted.

Over time, successful organizations grow and eventually require people whose sole purpose is to handle paperwork and internal affairs. Large organizations have external demands imposed upon them. The government is a major source of these demands, with laws about providing benefits, retirement plans, and job perquisites; labor markets and unions impose demands on how individuals move in and out of the organization. Large groups of people demand increasing amounts of fairness to all individuals involved, despite the fact that such growth prohibits satisfying all of the people all of the time. To ensure these demands are satisfied, organizations hire people just to administrate over them. These people literally only move paper around: into, out of, and within the organization.

This is not to imply that these individuals serve no purpose. Employees have to get paid, insurance claims have to be filed, incoming payments have to be processed, and endowments have to be nurtured. Somebody has to do it, and large organizations require individuals with special training who can handle the maze of paperwork. A structural engineer can't also be an expert in tax law and human resources. With bureaucrats in place, the organization is freed, in principle, to let each person do what they do best, rather than suffering the inefficiencies of multitasking. But as more time passes, the paper-pushers develop their own rules. They have to hire more people just to push around the extra paper that they generate to get the original papers pushed. They build a hierarchy and develop influence within the organization separate from the organization's original purpose. Now you have a bureaucracy.

Like any human system with self-interest, the focus of the bureaucracy is self-perpetuation. The bureaucracy is not there to introduce new products or find new customers. It exists only for internal consumption, and the lack of competition leads to incredible inefficiencies. For example, years after the Internet had become a standard feature of everyone's daily life, many universities still used paper-based systems for enrollment and course registration. Paper-based course registration gives the administrative bureaucracy power. They control what is on the paper, how it is filled out, and how it moves through the system. Moving to an online system means the bureaucracy loses power and the bureaucrats oppose it, no matter how efficient the change would be. Eventually, when a transition to an online system cannot be opposed any longer and to get the bureaucracy on board, the administration must argue that the new online system will serve or create a new IT bureaucracy.

And when such a new system is planned, it is first and foremost designed to appeal to the IT bureaucracy. It must be easy to administer. Usability for customers (i.e., the students) is a secondary concern. The more convoluted and confusing the implemented system, the more relevant the managing bureaucracy becomes and the more power it has. This is why such transitions, which seem obvious from the standpoint of usability and efficiency, take so long to implement and are implemented poorly when they finally are.

The careers of those who serve the bureaucracy depend on this infrastructure. Without the self-created maze of policies and regulations, which they alone are expert at navigating, they would have no other employable skills. Bureaucrats do not understand or care why the rules are the way they are; they only understand how to administer them. These rules endow them with power over others whom they could otherwise never control. It is human nature to desire domination and power, and the bureaucracy gives its adherents the ability to satisfy that need without having to risk face or fortune to obtain it. The bureaucrat does not view the bureaucracy as obstructive. They believe the bureaucracy brings order. Or, more probably, they don't care, as long as the job pays the bills. (How many people do you know say they want to work in human resources when they grow up?)

The bureaucrat has a process-driven mindset, rather than an outcome-driven one. The bureaucrat believes that the means justify the ends. As long as the rules have been followed, it doesn't matter what the outcome is. No individual bureaucrat is responsible for the generation of the rules or for their consequences; they simply carry them out, and the good or bad outcomes of their execution are out of their hands. Since everyone in the bureaucracy only carries out policy, no one is responsible for the outcomes. As long as protocol is followed, the bureaucrat doesn't care how many theses are left unsubmitted or loans not disbursed. It doesn't matter how crappy the course-registration software is, as long as it's implemented according to standard, satisfies the requirements, and all the proper signatures were had. The bureaucrats are expert at navigating the seas of red tape. For them, the process is their life. The rules and regulations offer structure and reduce uncertainty. More importantly, *the rules absolve the bureaucrat of responsibility*. A large company or institution has a dictionary-sized book of policies and practices, and any bureaucrat can always point to it and say they were only following orders.

The bureaucracy is strictly a cost center for a company or institution. Notwithstanding its value in keeping the organization running smoothly, the bureaucracy does not generate wealth; it only costs money. Scientists and engineers design new systems, services, and products for customers in new markets, but the bureaucracy never interacts with the money-making side of the business. Without it there would be no need for the bureaucracy at all, but the bureaucrats seldom see or influence the outcome of a company's projects. The bureaucracy may facilitate the generation of additional wealth (for example, by freeing up engineers to do engineering), but on every organization's ledger, the human resources department is always marked with red ink. The bureaucracy is a gigantic middle man, through which all activities must pass but which has no say in the creation or direction of those activities. There are no outcomes in bureaucracy, only process and perpetuation.

The Academic Track

In corporations, the bureaucracy serves the profit-seeking strategy laid out by executives. The VIPs in the board room set the ship's course, the employees keep the engines humming, and the bureaucracy keeps the crew fed, clothed, and insured. Although the bureaucracy wields power through its tyranny of red tape, it ultimately has little power to control which direction the company goes. Bureaucrats can be hired or fired at the whim of the markets and the company's profitability.

In academia, the inmates run the asylum: the people running the show are also bureaucrats. Universities do not have the same straightforward reason for existence that a company does. Universities have no profit motive (although they do, of course, seek increasing wealth). Educational goals are ambiguous and harder to quantify than revenues and profits, and universities lack a countervailing power to the bureaucracy. A university has no independent executives in a board room with a vested interest in the long-term profitability of a university (an academic board of trustees is seldom as financially invested in the state of a university as a corporate board is).

Professors are the source of new blood for the upper echelons of the academic bureaucracy. Almost universally it is academics who work their way up to dean, provost, bursar, registrar, and president. The hierarchy of adjunct professors, assistant professors, associate professors, and full professors splits into two directions: those who prefer research, and those who prefer administration. It may seem odd that a full professor in a technical discipline, perhaps with lots of grant money, would put so much of that success in stasis to take on an administrative job. However, for some people, administration is a more engaging calling. Not all professors are as wedded to their research as you might think. If you can imagine going into grad school because of inertia (as described in Chapter 1), you can also imagine continuing on to a professorship because of inertia. Administration can be a blessed escape from the rat race of grant writing and paper publishing.

Most professors are required to serve on committees, especially if they are seeking tenure. The committees give professors their first taste of being part of the bureaucracy, rather than opposing it. Their decisions on a committee can lead to major structural changes in curriculum, student life, tuition and fees, and other facets of academic life. Many professors consider the committees a chore, but others find attractive the opportunity to exert such influence. The committees also serve the bureaucracy: they shift responsibility for major decisions from the paper-pushing bureaucrats to an entire body of people, most of whom are tenured and can't be fired over the outcomes of their decisions.

The first administrative, bureaucratic position that a professor holds is the department head. Most true researchers view this position as a headache more than opportunity, and the pool of volunteers may be quite small. The department head represents the department to the public by appearing at recruitment events and interacting with prospective students, and to the rest of the university by sitting on higher-level committees and by being the point of contact for budgeting, regulating, and policy decisions.

The department head manages the budget, a thankless task that involves more grief than it deserves. He or she determines how many teaching positions can be paid for, how many fellowships go out and for how much, whether more faculty can be hired, and how much petty cash can be spread out for department events. No one can ever make a budget that makes most people happy; he or she must simply hope to anger the smallest number of people possible.

The head also makes the final decision for sundry minor matters, which always seem to cause more vicious battles in the academic bubble than money ever does: who gets an office, how big an office someone gets, who gets kicked out of an office, how many support staff can be hired, who gets a new computer, who has to share a lab. The head has great influence as the person responsible for setting up committees, but the head is also hamstrung by the department's tendencies to demand uniform approval of anything the committees recommend. The head cannot really get anything done without support of the tenured faculty.

Above department heads are the deans, which come in every shape and color. If there is a hierarchy to be managed, a dean will be appointed to manage it. Departments are usually parts of Divisions or Schools, which each have a dean. Divisions and Schools are parts of Colleges, which each have a dean. The Colleges make up a university, which has many miscellaneous deans plus a president and other bureaucrats. Every corner of the academic bureaucracy is filled with deans: a Dean of Students, a Dean of Faculty, a Dean of Student Life, a Dean for Business Development, a Dean for Study Abroad, a Dean for Professional Development and Community Engagement, a Dean for Equity, Diversity, & Inclusive Affairs. They are the bloated middle management of a university's administration.

Deans control the budgets that flow down to the departments and make many of the final hiring decisions for faculty and for department heads. From the perspective of the grad student, the deans are full of sound and fury, signifying nothing. They are paid extremely well for ambiguous responsibilities, notwithstanding their administrative role of managing the budgets and strategy of their respective sub-dominions. They primarily impact the student body by setting up initiatives full of buzz words and by finding ways to impose new rules and regulations on the execution of your research or classes. The extraordinary expansion of mandatory training in the last several years, whether for research ethics or sexual harassment or diversity awareness, originates from the deans' offices.

At the top of the academic ladder are the super-deans: the registrar, the bursar, and the provost. The registrar's office is familiar to every student, undergrad and grad, although no one has ever seen him or her personally. The registrar is responsible for handling student records. When you submit GRE scores to your new university, sign up for classes, drop a class, get a grade, and graduate, all the paperwork goes through the registrar.

The money you pay for that paperwork goes through the bursar, the university's head treasurer. His or her office ensures that tuition is billed promptly, handles payment plans, processes incoming payments, and hunts you down if you fall behind on your bills. Why would a tenured professor of, say, philosophy be given what is essentially an accounting and finance leadership position for a multi-billion-dollar enterprise? Your guess is as good as mine.

The provost is the university's vice president; in a corporation, the provost would be the Chief Operating Officer. He or she oversees all of the academic affairs at the university, including curriculum and research. When new research initiatives are announced or the core curriculum for undergraduates is re-designed, it's the doings of the provost. The provost tweaks the knobs that control academic affairs at the university to ensure continued accreditation while keeping the institution on the cutting edge.

The summit of the academic route in the bureaucracy is the role of university president. Sometimes called a "chancellor" at large, multi-campus institutions, the president functions as the CEO of the university. The president balances the university's account sheet and, in a crunch, makes the hard decisions about what gets cut and how benefits are disbursed. The president is caught in a maze of self-imposed regulations and externally imposed government rules about how tuition and fees can be modified, who can and cannot be fired, and how facilities can be used. While navigating these treacherous waters, the president is also answerable to the board of trustees. For all of this grief, however, the president is also paid very well, but probably less than the football coach.

The president establishes a vision and goals for the university and ostensibly implements a strategy for the university to accomplish those goals. Perversely, visions and goals in a bureaucratic setting are specifically defined as being ambiguous or unattainable. The "vision statement" is the gold at the end of the rainbow. The purpose of a vision statement is to describe a perfect world that the institution could bring about, a world that in reality can never be achieved. Goals are defined as steps towards that vision, although there is no quantifiable way to assert what or how many goals are necessary to achieve the vision or mission. The vision and goals set by the university president are conveniently designed to perpetuate the bureaucracy indefinitely. If a vision were reachable, the bureaucracy would have no reason to exist anymore.

The president serves as the public face of the university, although nobody except the rich and famous may actually see his or her face. While serving this political role, the president's main job is to raise money for the university and build the endowment. Universities, which are non-profit institutions, depend heavily on donations from wealthy alumni and benefactors to stay in business. Most of a president's time is spent on the road, hopping from capital drive to fundraiser to charity event, drumming up donations.

Like any CEO, a university president is judged by the growth and prosperity of the university. The president is a human, too,

and concerned about the progress of his or her career. A successful presidency can mean advancement to a larger and more
prestigious university, and to secure that new position often requires following the path of least resistance—or, the path of easiest measurement. Spearheading efforts to broadly improve academic standards or revamp the curriculum would be better for
students, but improvements in that area are hard to quantify, and
they don't significantly influence rankings in consumer-research
publications. On the other hand, the student-to-faculty ratio is
easy to measure and can directly affect a university's ranking.
When the money is there, hiring more faculty is an effective way
for a president to raise the bar.

Another easily measured metric is the student-to-treadmill ratio: put up a fancy new gym or student center and you have an instant photo opportunity that attracts more applications and low-
ers the acceptance rate, making the school appear more selective.
Putting up new buildings is also an easy way to look like you've
accomplished something. Whether you've increased the number
of classrooms is irrelevant. The president goes where the money
is and supports the construction of entrepreneurship centers, research labs, business incubators, and any other facilities that dramatically increase the university's square footage.

The Bureaucratic Track

Professors work their way up the academic track to become department heads, deans, provosts, and presidents. The bulk of the
administration at a university is made up of employees who start
entirely on the bureaucratic side and make a career of it. These
are the office workers at the registrar and bursar, the librarians,
the people in the housing office, and the secretaries who keep the
whole place running.

Departmental secretaries, the arm of the bureaucracy that a
grad student has the most interaction with, are a lesson in contra-
diction. You depend on them for everything, and they make the
wheels turn faster than if you tried on your own, but they are also
the most visible symptom of the bureaucracy. For every secretary
you interact with, there are two or three others who each have
their own office, but it is hard to tell what any of them actually

do.

The secretaries are the people you *must* have on your side. Most of the paperwork you file goes through them, they know the ins and outs of the bureaucratic hierarchy, and they have the skill to circumvent lots of rules regardless of what the official policy says. It is worth the time to develop positive relationships with the secretaries and to cultivate an especially close working relationship with one or two. These are the people you go to in a crunch or crisis. Academic bureaucrats are too busy to handle details, and they depend on the secretaries' judgment. If you have one gunning for you, a secretary can make things happen or make problems go away.

These secretaries tend to be less vested in the propagation of the bureaucracy, being at the bottom of the food chain. With a few secretary friends you can probably extricate yourself out of a paperwork jam. The best secretaries function as an interface between the desperate, outcome-oriented students, like those who need a hold taken off their registration, and the process-oriented bureaucracy working against them. Without the secretaries, grad students would have to know all the rules of the bureaucracy themselves.

Never take the secretaries for granted. This is an unfortunate habit among professors, who frequently boss secretaries around, give them mountains of busy work, and come at the last minute for every task. It is not uncommon to see a professor have a tantrum at a secretary, merely because they can. A secretary can be fired for a making a fuss, but a tenured professor is free to act as puerile as he or she wants.

The secretaries deserve your respect. Do what you can to make their life easier, and they will be willing to go the extra mile and make your life easier. Your interaction with a secretary should be similar to that with your advisor. Go as far as you can with a task by yourself, and approach the secretary for the exact help they can provide. Have a specific question or a clear idea of the information or help you need. Most importantly, always thank a secretary for their help. If they know you appreciate them, they will bump you to the head of the line ahead of cranky tenured faculty.

Interacting with the Bureaucracy

A grad student interacts with the bureaucracy every day in one way or another, even if it is just tapping into the power of the departmental secretaries to get around it. Every day you access buildings and log into computers that are part of the technology bureaucracy, which rules building hours, access rights, software licenses, and intellectual property rights. Every semester you interact with the bureaucracy while setting up your TA or RA appointments and registering for classes. When the time comes to graduate you have to fill out forms and submit to formatting and submission guidelines for your thesis. No matter how you cut it, you run into the academic bureaucracy every day. The best way to survive is to learn some of the unwritten rules that apply to every bureaucracy.

First and foremost: once you have something, never give it up. Possession is nine tenths of the bureaucracy. With the passage of time you will accumulate property and perquisites through the bureaucracy, whether it is office furniture, special sets of keys, or other privileges. Thanks to the typically crossed lines of communication, you may find yourself in possession of an office with a window or a fancy, expensive chair: the sort of premium accommodations a grad student isn't supposed to have. It's not hard to game the system to get your hands on these sorts of things. Once you finally do have it, however, it is very hard to lose it. If you stick to your guns, the bureaucracy has almost no means to take back what they've given away.

In the department where I studied, desks and offices were assigned only to grad students with funding, whether through a TA, an RA, or a fellowship. I knew many students who, being funded for one semester, were given space in an office, but who never left when they failed to secure a TA position the next semester. Once those students are in place, they become lost in the system, and it is very difficult for the bureaucracy to evict them. You shouldn't give up your office without a fight, whether you're funded or not. It is easier for the bureaucracy to just leave you alone and carry on.

You also must never fear to use the university's bloat against itself. The bureaucracy is accustomed to intimidating the serfs that it claims to serve, especially undergrads with no money or power. Bureaucrats have no more power than you; they only have the power of red tape. If you get to know the policies and practices yourself, you can use them against the bureaucracy. Citing the scripture of regulation when you want something leaves the bureaucracy unable to resist.

Despite the reverence for rules and regulations, a great deal of activity in the academic bureaucracy is unofficial, done off the books. Tuition wavers, funding levels, and employment contracts for TAs and RAs are often not written down. For example, there may be a general agreement on the process for accepting a TA position, but you may find that after being assigned a TA slot you never actually sign anything aside except an income-tax form. This lackadaisical approach to paperwork can work in everyone's favor: it leaves you lots of negotiating room and gives the administration flexibility. On the other hand, you are left with no guarantees about how you will be treated. This atmosphere of uncertainty motivates the creation of grad-student labor unions.

When the bureaucracy does write something down, you must hold them to it. A fellow grad student of mine once received his acceptance letter to the program that included a guarantee of four years of TA funding. A guarantee of that nature was unorthodox, but once it was down on paper, there was nothing the department could do. Two years later, when budgets tightened and the administration threatened to cut back TA positions (including his), he was able to pull out his letter. The letter hadn't been drafted by a lawyer. It had no warnings or stipulations about the availability of future funding. It was a blanket guarantee. The bureaucracy had been hoisted with its own petard.

If the grinding inefficiency of the bureaucracy blocks something that you are legally entitled to, the bureaucracy will fold in an instant when threatened with legal action. The university's reputation is its most precious asset: it is the key to draw new students and it is the key to its prestige. Getting embroiled in lawsuits with students over trifling matters is bad business. Threatening to call a lawyer is an option of last resort, but sometimes it is necessary, and the bureaucracy knows well when it is at fault. In the example above with a letter of "guaranteed" TA employment, it could be argued that the letter was legally binding based on who wrote it and how it motivated a student's decision to attend the university. If the school had persisted in cutting his TA position, he would have had a substantial case against them. It is unlikely it would ever come to that, but the option is there when all other hopes have been extinguished.

The most important thing to remember when you interact with the bureaucracy is that all rules are flexible. The bureaucracy is a creation of man, and so too are its rules and regulations. Nothing in the bureaucracy is a law of physics. If you find the person with enough power, you can get anything done regardless of what the rules say is proper. A secretary at the bottom of the food chain can help you get around a paperwork deadline, and a dean at the top can waive rules about scheduling your thesis defense. If you treat the rules of the bureaucracy like they're real laws, the bureaucracy will rule you. The rules create a system of behavior to make *administrators'* lives easier. Learn to play the game, make the right connections, bend the rules that you can, and never fear to ask for an exception, and you can rule (or at least survive) the bureaucracy.

Chapter 10

Getting a Job

After years of effort working towards your M.S. or Ph.D., your moment has come: graduation. With cameras flashing and a proud family looking on, a smiling dean meets you on stage, hands you a leather-bound diploma, and ushers you into the ranks of the unemployed.

After years of living on the salary of a TA or RA, the university can't and won't feed you any longer. That fancy degree makes you more expensive, and with your graduation to "professional" status comes the expectation of employment benefits and treatment as a human being, rather than as a penniless student. Many books cover the post-graduation job hunt, and I cannot hope to top them in the space of one chapter. Instead, this chapter offers a few nuggets of advice on finding a professional position in the sciences and engineering, and in a bit more frank fashion than other sources may provide.

After graduation, one is first struck by the jarring realization that there is no "next step" expected of you on the path of your life. Your career is starting, and every person's career is different. You are faced with few if any necessary steps moving forward. To this point in your life, the path from elementary school to high school to college to grad school has been laid out for you. When you leave grad school and start a job (even if you stay in academia as a post-doc or professor), no one will tell you what to do with your life. No one will stop you from running off and joining a commune. If you take the first job you can and stay in the same

191

position for forty years and then retire, no one will comment. You can stay in your field, or do something completely different, provided you can get someone to pay you. Grad school is a great way to put off real life, but you can't put it off any longer. A decision must be made about your future. A job? A post-doc? A faculty position? You must do *something*, because you have to eat. The decision you make at the end of grad school may not be final, as life is long and has many twists and turns, but will affect the course of your life for several years after.

Before you graduate, perhaps an entire year before, is the time to begin the process of finding a new position. You must prepare your resume and submit job applications. You built a professional network in grad school by attending conferences and hob-nobbing with the well-connected, and now is the time to massage that network to find out who is hiring. Finding a job is one reason you have a network in the first place, and asking for favors is part of the networking process. By the time you defend your Ph.D. or master's degree, most of the legwork of finding a job should be done, and most students already have their next position lined up by graduation. In fact, some grad students start a job months before they officially finish their degree. These lucky individuals write up their dissertation while working at their new, full-time job.

Your Resume and CV

Your resume is one of the most important documents you will compose in your life, and you will update it frequently over the course of your career. Your resume is the only information that future employers initially have to sort the wheat from the chaff as they seek to fill open positions. This is the place to shine as brightly as possible by ensuring that your skills align with an employer's needs and that all the buzz words are on the front page to get you into the coveted "interview" pile.

There are two types of resumes, and you may need to write both during the job search: the standard resume, which is used for seeking jobs in industry and government, and the *curriculum vitae* or CV, which is used primarily by Ph.D.'s to catalog academic achievements and for seeking jobs in academia. You may see the word "resume" used generically for either the standard resume or the CV.

Your resume must above all look professional: the format for a resume may not be standardized, but if it looks carelessly constructed, you'll never pass the smell test. A potential employer should not be the proof reader for your resume, and that starts with paying attention to spelling and grammar. Anecdotes abound of hiring managers reading resumes of highly educated graduates with poor punctuation, rampant misspellings, and sentences that read like a fifth-grade book report. These resumes are immediately dispatched to the circular filing bin.*

Even so, the resume is no place to demonstrate your ability to write stirring prose. Complete sentences are few and far between in the brief space that you have to tell the reader about yourself and your skills. Bullets points, bold-face headings, and sentence fragments rule the day. Find a friend, preferably more than one, who can read your resume long before you submit it to a company. It's better to embarrass yourself to your roommate with bad spelling than to someone you want to give you a paycheck.

It also may be worth composing your resume in a professional typesetting format like LaTeX, especially if you have the skills from months of thesis-writing. Most applicants preparing a resume resort to Microsoft Word and, worse, to its default settings. Dozens of resumes pass a hiring manager's desk, all laid out with the same font, color, and heading styles that Bill Gates selected for them. A fancier system like LaTeX adds an extra touch of class, and its vast array of typesetting options can make your resume stand out from the others.

All resumes of technically trained individuals have the same general content, but there is no standard format. Each resume is designed to appeal to each employer and to apply to the position being filled. Some sections may be moved, some deleted, and others bulked up with more detail to emphasize special skills. Your resume is broken up into distinct sections, each demarcated unambiguously with heading text, which facilitates consumption by overworked employers. Topics that show up in your resume (extra items for a CV are discussed later) include:

---

*That is, the trash can.

1. **Contact info.** Were you one of those kids in elementary school who always forgot to put your name on homework before handing it in? It is more common than you'd expect, so don't let the habit follow you to your resume. In the excitement of listing your life's accomplishments, it is easy to forget the most important information of all: how to contact you. An employer must be able to find you with multiple redundant options. Include both your home and work (i.e. university) address, a phone number (home and office), email address, and even a fax number if your university department lets you. Now is the time to get a professional-sounding and -looking email address. In grad school you might get away with partydude@awesome.com, but your resume demands something more understated, or just use your university email.

2. **Citizenship.** Many technical fields are sensitive for reasons of national security, and employers may require US citizenship for employment. However, it is legally dubious (if not outright illegal) to ask about your citizenship status. You can save an employer a lot of trouble by telling them outright whether you are a US citizen. It's nothing that you would be secretive about anyway, and if you're not a US citizen the employer will find out eventually.

3. **Objective.** This is a one- or two-sentence description of the position you are seeking or the type of work you want to do. You know very well what job you want, but the employer doesn't. Do you want a full-time position or part-time? Do you want to do technical analysis or management? This brief statement, not dissimilar from a personal ad in a newspaper, lays out for the reader what you expect out of the application process. The line "I seek a full-time technical position in the biotechnology industry where I can contribute my skills to the design and prototyping of new artificial joints and implants" tells the employer several things to help sort you into the proper bin for hiring: looking for a "full-time" position has salary implications, a "technical" position means you are probably interested in exercising your science or engineering skills rather than going into management, "design

and prototyping" signals an interest in research and development rather than manufacturing, and "artificial joints and implants" hones down on your particular expertise or interest. Specificity is key. Avoid ambiguous and trite platitudes about being a "dynamic" and "people-oriented" go-getter looking to "engage" your "synergistic" skills in a "challenging but rewarding" environment. Lines like that say nothing substantive about you and make you look like you yourself don't know what you want to do.

4. **Education.** Credentials are extremely important in the hiring process—whether you've actually been educated or not—and for those of us leaving grad school without having had a real job before (except maybe some internships), the education section of your resume is the only place an employer can gauge your future performance. For every academic degree you have (that is, starting with undergraduate), you should include the name of the degree, the date, the institution, and your major. If you have extra honors associated with the degree (like *magna cum laude*) or thesis titles, those belong on your resume as well. For young graduates without work experience, you should include your GPA for each degree. Although getting an advanced degree has minimum GPA requirements anyway, you will inevitably find many employers asking for it, and it's better to have your GPA ready for them on the page than make them write it down by hand or have to follow up with it later.

5. **Work Experience.** The names of your former employers and the years you worked for them belong here, as does a brief and pithy description of your responsibilities and accomplishments. You should be specific about your jobs with previous employers and sum up in a sentence or two what you did, how you exercised your skills, and how you succeeded in your assigned tasks. Much as with the "Objective" section above, avoid ambiguous language or generic job descriptions. A "lab assistant" generically "supports ongoing research and development," which everyone already knows and says nothing about your responsibilities. It is much more impressive and indicative of your skills if you

write, "designed new knee-joint replacement hardware currently under review for human testing." Someone who has past experience is cheaper to hire and train, and tailoring the description of your past employment to emphasize experience is the best way to get attention. If you haven't had a real job yet, you should include your internships and research-related work as an undergraduate or grad student. Any time you were paid to perform a task and gained a skill counts as work experience, whether as a paid intern in industry or working as an RA.

6. **Other skills.** As you developed your technical skills in class, you inevitably picked up many others that don't fit neatly into "work" or as part of your degree but that nonetheless make you more employable. Computer skills are at the top of the list, including the operating systems you know how to use (e.g., having experience with Unix or Linux in the sciences and engineering is a big plus), programming languages you know (everything from C to HTML to MATLAB), and specialized software, especially software with a sharp learning curve, like Adobe Photoshop and AutoCAD. Foreign languages are another skill to list in your resume. With a global economy, having one or two other languages under your belt makes you marketable to a wider array of employers and could even get you into jobs that involve foreign junkets!

The organization of your resume depends on what you want to emphasize. Education and work experience always appear first, but after that you can modify the order of the content to suit the potential employer. If you're applying for a job that involves a lot of computer programming, computer skills should be posted front and center, but if you're applying to a multinational conglomerate, foreign languages might belong first in line.

The cousin to the resume is the CV, the *curriculum vitae*, which means "course of life" in Latin. Whereas your resume is a document focused on highlighting particular skills for a particular position, your CV is a complete biography of your professional existence, documenting every degree, publication, award, and speck of experience you pick up over the course of your life. The CV is an absolute requirement for seeking academic positions, as it contains more detail on academic achievements and publications than is appropriate on a one- or two-page resume. Regardless of the position you seek or the career track you pursue, everyone with a Ph.D. should have a CV at the ready. Industry may never require or care about it, but after building up a long academic pedigree towards your Ph.D., it is valuable to keep track of your accomplishments. When you have need for a resume, you can pare down the extensive CV to the facts you need for the occasion.

A CV looks like a grossly expanded resume. All of the items listed above for the resume are still required, but several other sections also belong, sometimes near the front of the line (I continue the numbering scheme from before):

7. **Skills and thesis.** Some resumes have an objective, which describes your employment goals, and you can complement the objective by outright listing the technical skills you have and, for good measure, describe your thesis in a short paragraph. A single job opening may have dozens of applicants, and reviewers don't want to decipher your skills from long lists of honors, teaching, and publications. Give them what they want up front: a list of what you know how to do. For some positions it may be fine to list "organic chemistry" as a skill, even though it is really a subject. On the other hand, if organic chemistry experience is a *sine qua non* for a job at a pharmaceutical giant, more specific skills like "spectroscopy" and "chromatography" may be more appropriate.

8. **Publications.** The pinnacle of academic achievement is enshrinement in an archived journal, and your CV documents each example with your name on it. Your papers are listed chronologically by year (ascending or descending is up to you), and you should include papers both where you are first author and where you are not. Try to make the first paper on your list one where you are the first author, if possible, and it may take some maneuvering to maintain a chronological listing. Conference papers should be listed in a separate section from journal articles. Academic positions in particular often do not "count" conference papers, and they should not

be mixed with the journals. Conference posters can also be listed, if they (or their associated abstracts) are archived, and any patents in your name are also appropriate. You can also include invited publications or other miscellaneous credits, such as encyclopedia articles, magazine articles, textbooks, or photo credits.

9. **Honors and awards.** Industry has occasional achievement awards, but academia thrives on the pomp of medals, certificates, and honors that recognize your accomplishments, from the most profound to the most mundane, and all of them belong on your CV. You should include scholarships and fellowships, teaching awards, academic honors, scholarly prizes, and any other sort of official recognition that comes your way. Many of the items you list may seem trivial, but they count for a lot in the process of candidate selection and salary calculation. For better or worse, honors beget more honors, and individuals reviewing a CV may expect to see a self-sustaining reaction of awards. Lacking a trail of honors and awards may signal (rightly or wrongly) that you have not distinguished yourself from the rest of the pack.

10. **Teaching experience.** Few people in industry will care about your time as a TA or course instructor in grad school, but applying for an academic position means applying first and foremost to be an educator. Capable students with superb grades do not necessarily make good teachers, and grades cannot be enough to secure a teaching position. One should have the experience of leading a classroom and developing a curriculum to secure a teaching position at a university. The teaching experience you list can include TA positions, courses you instructed in grad school, and even tutoring jobs: anything that demonstrates you not only know the content, but also have some skill at communicating it to others. You should list not only what classes you taught and your title (e.g., TA vs. instructor), but also your specific responsibilities. Did you help develop part of the syllabus? Did you make the homework and exams yourself? Did you lecture in a classroom, meet with students in small groups,

or one-on-one? There are many facets to the teaching experience, and you should demonstrate in your CV that you
have at least been exposed to all of them.

11. **Professional societies.** A professional engineer or scientist
    is expected to be a member of one or more professional so-
    cieties. Membership is required to present at conferences
    sponsored by a society, and their presence on your resume
    suggests active participation in the community (although
    most people don't use their memberships beyond attending
    the conferences).

12. **Graduate-level classes.** For the young graduate, there may
    be little work experience to list. Lacking a 5- or 10-year
    history of professional accomplishment and responsibility
    (except for your thesis), it is hard to convey the skills you
    have. If you are fresh out of grad school, you may consider
    including—at the end of your CV—a list of the graduate-
    level classes you completed and their content. Do not list
    the official course description, which is often bland and am-
    biguous, but rather the specific topics covered in the syl-
    labus. Sometimes a company or institution is looking for
    people with exposure to very particular subjects, and they
    may pop up in your list of classes.

The proper length of your resume or CV is a matter of perpetual debate. There are those who insist that no resume should
exceed a single page, lest a poorly stapled document fall apart
or a reviewer risk a paper cut by turning a page. In response
to this conventional wisdom, many one-page resumes have been
stretched to absurd extremes: microscopic font sizes, descriptions
of former jobs trimmed so short they are barely coherent, and page
margins measured in nanometers. For the sake of cramming in as
much material as possible, readability suffers and the resume is
more cumbersome than if it had been left on two pages.

When you submit a short resume of one or two pages, you
must cut to the bone. Highlight the bare essentials and make your
point to the reader. You need to convey two things: why would
someone want to hire you, and how do your skills match the requirements in the job description? If you cut out every hint of fluff

and address just those questions, it should be possible to get your entire life reduced down to a single page.

Whether you need a CV or a resume, you should maintain a long-form version, with all of the details, history, honors, credits, and skills, from which you can cherry pick to create the short resumes you need. When you apply for a job, you can submit the long and short forms. The short resume goes at the top of the pile: the document you physically hand to an interviewer. The long resume is a supplemental document, which you can hand over for an interviewer to read later. When they have the time, they may peruse your eight-page behemoth.

Employers read a lot of resumes: make it easy to find what the reviewer needs by tailoring your resume to each application and to human nature. People who have to read lots of resumes won't be reading critically. They gravitate towards bold-face font, short lines, and brief quotes. Give them what they want, and everyone is happy. After you do a few interviews, you'll get a feel for the information that employers in your industry need. One interviewer may want to see your GPA, another may look for your years of experience. Regardless of how important you feel this information is or not, accommodating *them* will streamline the hiring process.

Your advisor has seen many students move out of the research group and on to employment of various kinds, and he can provide plenty of advice on crafting your resume. He likely has an excellent gauge on what employers like to see in your field. Your university's career office is also a valuable resource for the resume-writing process. Counselors there make a living by refining students' resumes into a standard that is accepted by the business community, and they provide proof-reading services to assess the content of your resume and CV.

When you submit your resume, it is common for an employer to also request a cover letter. In contrast to your resume, which is a cold and quantitative outline of your potential value to a company, the cover letter is a chance to describe yourself and your value in plain English. The cover letter never exceeds one page, and is formatted as a formal letter with a handful of eloquent but candid paragraphs. A cover letter describes who you are, where you come from professionally, what sort of position you seek, and why you are interested in their particular company. Every job description has a list of required or recommended skills, and the cover letter gives you the chance to highlight how you satisfy them. Explicitly lay out the items in the job description and elaborate in prose how your experiences make you the perfect person for the job. The cover letter provides a human connection to the impersonal pedigree in your resume. Your university's career office and the Internet have thousands of cover letter examples to peruse and to use as models for your own.

As a brief aside, keep in mind that your resume, CV, and cover letter are not legally binding documents. Exaggeration, manipulation, and whitewashing are common in the real world, and every employer reads a resume with a small grain of salt. In practice, you can put anything you want on your resume, including your former jobs as pope, invincible superhero, and alligator wrangler. If, somehow, that baloney still gets you a job interview, you'll have to fill out a completely separate document, provided by the hiring company, which *is* legally binding. The career information you provide in that document is what circulates around the company and what determines hiring and salary decisions.

The Job Fair

When your resume or CV is ready (long, short, or otherwise), you can start shopping it around. Most universities hold job fairs once or twice per semester, and these events are an excellent opportunity to get eyeballs on your resume, both for job-search purposes and to get feedback on your resume while you're still in control (as opposed to sending it off into the ether of online job postings). Job fairs stack the odds in your favor because companies come there specifically on a mission to do some hiring (or at least find interview candidates) and to get word out about their great company.

Strategic preparation for a large student job fair is as important as it is for a conference. Read the list of attending companies ahead of time and prioritize whom you want to visit. At a large university, there may be thousands of students coming to the fair, and you can bet that there will be long lines at the big-name companies. There is only so much time in the day: you have to budget how long you are willing to stand in line for Boeing when you could visit three other smaller companies' booths in the same time. You'll need a stack of your short resume to hand off in vast quantities at each booth you visit. Cover letters and long resumes can be kept in reserve, but it may not be prudent to hand those over right away. Recruiters operate on a "just the facts, ma'am" basis.

You also should have an "elevator pitch" ready. The elevator pitch is a one- or two-minute speech that summarizes everything you think an employer would want to know, such as your academic background, skills, position sought, and why you're interested in them. You may not get through the whole thing as conversation takes over, but you need it ready to go. Recruiters meet a lot of people each day, and it's hard to keep track of everyone. You will distinguish yourself by honing your pitch to crisp and memorable sound bites. Just because a recruiter is representing his or her company at the fair doesn't mean they're stellar conversationalists. It is your responsibility to drive the conversation, and the content of your elevator pitch fills in awkward silences.

If a meeting at a job-fair booth goes well, you may be invited to attend a one-on-one interview later that day or the next. Whereas meetings at the booth are mostly a hand-shaking event and a resume hand-over, these interviews offer employers the chance to learn more about the most promising candidates, especially those under consideration for full employment. That interview, usually at a time and place of the company's choosing (and frequently somewhere in the bowels of the university's career office), is the time for you to bring a cover letter and long resume along. Hand them over when you meet to provide the interviewer more material to chew on and to aide conversation; without it, the recruiter may be left with nothing but bland pro forma questions from the company. This on-site interview is not a "real" interview, as they cannot make a decision to hire you then and there. Rather, it provides enough content for the recruiter to return home and know to whom to send your resume on. He or she scans, copies, or emails your resume to managers most appropriate for your skills and experience level. Only then does the real process of a job application begin.

The Industry Path

In the sciences and engineering, industry is the most common final destination for graduates, offering the most variety and far more remuneration for your effort. Compared to academia, work in government and industry is less flexible: you work five days a week on a regular schedule and with limited vacation time. Industry also offers substantially less job security; at a university with a tenure-track (or better, tenured) position, it's very hard to lose your job, but a private company has the power to terminate your employment at any time. In return, though, you are paid better at the start of employment and the heights are much higher to which you can rise.

Some industries require time in a post-doc before you can get a full-time position, especially in the biomedical and pharmaceutical industries. This post-doc could be satisfied at a university, but many companies have post-docs of their own internally, funded through federal research grants. These corporate post-docs certainly pay better than those in academia and function as a sort of junior position within the company, after which you would very likely be promoted to a full-time, full-responsibility position.

Barring any other such prerequisites, the application process for a regular job is fairly uniform. Finding available positions in industry involves the two tried-and-true avenues: published postings and your professional network. Personal connections are far more likely to get you an interview than anything else. If you or your advisor knows someone who works at a company that interests you, send them a copy of your resume, whether there are posted openings or not. They can shop you and your resume around on the inside.

If you have no personal contact for a job opportunity, job fairs and online postings are the most common source. Each field has its mammoth companies that are constantly hiring, but there are many smaller companies out there waiting for talented graduates to come calling. Although you may not expect to take a job at a smaller concern, getting interviews and offers from as many companies as possible gives you experience and leverage when negotiating an offer.

For every field or job you are interested in, you can make a broad search of companies that do that sort of work, thinking broadly about terminology. You may think of your field in terms of "orbits," but not every company may use that word for similar positions. It may take searching for "trajectory" and "dynamics" to build a broader base of companies to start with. You can also consider companies that need your skills but that may not be in your immediate field. A degree in aerodynamics is obvious for Boeing or Airbus, but car companies and wind-turbine manufacturers also need aerodynamicists.

Most companies have an online form or system to apply to a specific job solicitation. Your vital information is uploaded with a cover letter, resume, and any other documents that they or you want to send. Even with an online system, if you have a personal contact within the company you should send your resume in through that person as well. Managers doing the hiring often need you "officially" in the system through the online application, regardless of your direct interaction with them.

If your resume attracts the right attention—a process that may take weeks or months if you have no one to accelerate the process for you from the inside—you may advance to the next level of interest: the phone call. Having reviewed your resume and decided you are a promising candidate, a potential boss calls you (or, emails you to set up the phone interview). This is a call for your boss to get to know you beyond the skills listed impersonally in your resume and the rampant self-promotion of a cover letter. She needs to know how interested you are in the position: many qualified people apply for positions that they have no intention of accepting, and the phone interview is a painless way for management to weed out the most obviously uninterested candidates.

The phone interview usually goes well, particularly if you show plenty of enthusiasm for the company and the job. If the manager likes you, they'll commit and bring you in for an on-site interview. The company flies you in at their expense, puts you up in a hotel, and invites you to their facility to meet the team. The on-site interview, given the cost and investment on the company's part, is a good sign that you're going to get an offer. Most positions in technical fields are filled on a strategic basis by selecting the most promising candidate, as opposed to fielding a large number of interviewees and choosing thereafter. They bring you in when they think you're a good fit, which means you're 85% of the way there.

The on-site interview is a chance for the people in the com-

pany to get to know you. Under most circumstances, your qual-
ifications are a done deal. Your resume thoroughly covers your
technical capabilities, and you wouldn't be invited for an interview if it wasn't already obvious you had the technical chops to
fill the position. The question instead is whether your potential
co-workers think they can work with you and whether you would
fit in at the company. You aren't there to impress them with your
technical skill, so be yourself. Be affable and personable. Be the
person that you would want to work with.

Your day at the company involves a marathon of interviews,
possibly interspersed with tours and visits of the company's facilities. You may end up interviewing with a dozen people over
the day, each for a half hour or so, and conversation may be about
technical material or about the weather, depending on the individual.

Use these interviews to your advantage and ask as many questions as possible. Accepting a position at the company is going
to affect *your* life a lot more than it will affect your boss or future
coworkers. You need to ask about the work environment, company culture, the housing market, the social scene, and all of the
other facets of the job and the area that will affect your quality
of life. A day of this process is exhausting, but by the end of the
day your store of questions and your energy should be utterly de-
pleted. You need to have enough information to decide whether
you're willing to commit to several years of working and living
there.

When the interview day is over, it's time to go home. It is possible that the manager will tell you they want to give you an offer,
but that is by no means guaranteed. If not, you return home and
wait. Even if your boss wants to offer you a job, it's not her who
can actually make an offer. The offer comes through human resources after a protracted and mystic process out of the hands of
your immediate management.

The job hunt is not fun, it's not easy, and it involves a lot of
soul-searching, weighing the pros and cons of salary, geography,
and office culture. The job that you accept will probably be with
you for several years and can dramatically affect the direction of
your career. It is not a task to take lightly. Start the process as early
as possible, and give yourself plenty of time to make a decision.

Remember, a company hires you because they will make more

money from your work than what they pay you. Don't feel pressured into making a snap judgment on something so important. Make your choice when you're ready, and take care that the job you take is one that you want (or as close to it as you can get). No amount of money can offset the misery of a job you hate.

The Academic Path

To put it bluntly, if you want to follow the academic path for your career, you need to be damned sure about it. The path is long, arduous, thankless, stressful, treacherous, and poorly paid. The professional side of the academic world has many warts that your time in grad school gradually reveals. Your advisor's face is streaked with stress lines, induced from years of writing grant applications on a midnight deadline, negotiating with the university bureaucracy for the proper facilities, and filling up his own CV with publications to seize that most sought-after treasure, tenure. If, despite the warning signs on the road ahead, you are still attracted to the luxuries of a flexible lifestyle, secure employment (at least post-tenure), and pushing the frontiers of human knowledge, the academic life might be for you. Alas, securing that academic life is no picnic, and finishing your Ph.D. is only the start of the process.

A Ph.D. is a non-negotiable minimum for nearly all academic positions, and before you seek a faculty position it is common (if not absolutely necessary) to seek a post-doctoral position, in which you take the role of "professor-in-waiting." Post-docs take on many administrative responsibilities of a research lab, managing its day-to-day operations while the PI is off around the world ginning up more support and being all-around important. The post-doc functions as a professor apprentice. As a grad student you were focused on research and getting your advanced degree, which did not inherently require your moving on to an academic position. Even at the level of an M.S. or Ph.D., most of the managerial tasks of a large research group are concealed. In most fields, accepting a post-doc position signals a commitment to the academic life, and a new phase of training begins when you learn how academia really works.

A post-doc is applied for much like a regular job. Solicitations are posted on professors' websites and in scholarly magazines, but your best bet is through the grapevine. Your advisor has contacts at other universities who are looking for new and reliable recruits, and if you've built up your own network over the years, you should have at least a few names you can call. If the hiring PI approves, you'll get hired into the lab and handed lots of responsibility right off the bat, perhaps managing a gaggle of new grad students. A post-doc is paid a bit more than a grad-student RA, but not excessively so: the academic path is no way to get rich. You'll become involved with the PI in the process of grant writing and designing research strategy. Your PI initiates you into the secret art of writing grants that push the right buttons to get noticed and that appeal to funding-committee members. While you manage part or all of a lab, you continue research yourself. Your post-doc is the time to isolate the specific area of research you want to pursue for a career and to start making a name for yourself. Getting publications are paramount so that you can credibly seek a faculty position at the end of your post-doc.

The tenure-track position is the goal of anyone on the academic path, but prerequisites for seeking such a position vary depending on field. Many departments will not consider you unless you've done a few years of a post-doc at other universities, building up your experience base. A respectable collection of publications is a must; if you were especially prolific in grad school, you might be able to apply for a tenure-track position fresh out of your Ph.D. (especially when your research doesn't require a lab).

News of open faculty positions comes from other faculty at your university or through the publications of professional societies. If you thumb through the last half-dozen pages of a society's quarterly circular, you are bound to find a number of long and detailed announcements of opening positions. These solicitations include a description of the university and department and outline the area of expertise they seek in a new faculty member. This field-of-study constraint is flexible if you are a competitive candidate, and you should seriously consider any announcement that even tangentially aligns with your own field.

Before you apply for every faculty position in the back of a magazine, you need to get as much information as possible about the university in question. If it is a large university, there may be an undue emphasis on research dollars at the expense of eloquence or teaching ability. Can you expect to bring in enough money to keep your position and get tenure? Some fields don't have a lot of money and can't get a foothold at large institutions. Smaller universities may have more emphasis on teaching and professor-student interaction; if you prefer research over pedagogy, these people-oriented institutions may not be for you. You should get to know a department's strengths and weaknesses, information readily available through its website. All of the professors and their fields of expertise are listed there. Are there already two or three professors in your field? Or is there something new that you can contribute?

If you are part of the fortunate few who are invited for an interview at the university, you will be led around to meet many (if not all) of the faculty, who size you up. Academic politics is a dangerous game, and you should be as uncontroversial as possible. Every department is a minefield of discontent, and you never know what offhand comment might disqualify you. If you stick to your story about research and accomplishments and ask lots of questions yourself, you'll be far better off than if you spend too much time pontificating on academic politics and bureaucracy.

The academic interview also includes a colloquium, where you present the fruits of your grad-student or post-doc labor to an audience of faculty and students. This presentation is your chance to demonstrate your communication skills, and it may be the only opportunity for the decision makers to assess your suitability for the classroom. Many applicants stumble in the colloquium, either because they are underprepared or because they really aren't good communicators. The students in attendance will be very frank in their opinions to the faculty, and their word can carry a lot of weight. The colloquium is your time to shine, and a dazzling presentation can clinch that coveted position.

The demand for academic positions has increased dramatically in the last few decades, outstripping the supply at chronically under-funded universities. Departments cannot muster the funding to hire the full-time, tenure-track faculty necessary to satisfy demand from newly minted Ph.D.'s or to man ever-growing undergraduate lectures. Instead, you may find yourself offered an "adjunct" or "visiting" position, a no-man's land where you have the power and authority of a professor, but where you can never achieve tenure and are not part of the permanent faculty.

An adjunct's contract is year-to-year and could be severed at any moment, whereas a tenure-track assistant professor is guaranteed four or five years before the tenure chopping block. The adjunct position offers much less pay than a tenure-track professor and may not even be classified as a full-time position, thereby freeing the university from having to offer any benefits. Alas, in today's competitive world, an adjunct or visiting position may be the only opportunity available and is still far superior to being unemployed.

Epilogue: Social Life

Writing about social life in grad school feels a bit like writing fiction. You're not supposed to have a social life, right? Grad school is like joining an academic seminary: vows of poverty and chastity, plus a commitment of service and labor to the almighty PI. There should be no time for a social life, an unholy temptation that diverts grad students from the path of scholarly righteousness.

Unfortunately, some grad students believe this propaganda, which generations of advisors have promoted because they have more use for you toiling in lab than enjoying a weekend barbecue. Wander any academic building on a Saturday night and you will find more than a few offices lit, where tired grad students hunch over their desks grading papers or writing conference abstracts. Further down the hall, the silver hum of fluorescent lighting fills labs where grad students tend to their rats and squeeze in a few extra experiments while the building is quiet. These grad students are anonymous, because they rarely interact with anyone: they come to the office or lab in mid-morning, keep to their own bench at work, eat by themselves, go home around midnight, get four or five hours of sleep, and repeat the cycle for the duration of their M.S. or Ph.D. No one has a conversation with them that isn't about research, if you can corner them long enough to speak more than two words. And although their unkempt hair, sunken eyes, and twitching limbs attest to a life of perpetual exhaustion and Ramen-induced malnutrition, you can't help but feel a twinge of guilt that maybe *you* should be that devoted to your research, too.

Contrary to this prevailing wisdom, grad school does not require the sacrifice of your physical and mental well-being. You should—must!—cultivate a social life. Your life is not over be-

211

cause you begin grad school; you're just on one of life's little de-
tours. In fact, this may be one of the last times in your life when
you have substantial amounts of free time and a flexible schedule.
After this, it's 40 or more hours per week on the job with precious
little vacation time.

Interaction with other human beings is what keeps most of us
mentally healthy, and it is all too easy to leave friendships behind
at the start of grad school. Most of us transfer to a new school
where we know no one, and unlike in undergrad, the university
has no programs to enforce socialization among grad students.
You may keep in touch with friends from undergrad, but they are
moving on with life as much as you; your paths diverge over time,
and they won't serve your needs for day-to-day contact. At some
point you have to branch out and meet new people. Yes, socially
you're starting over again, just like those first days of freshman
year.

Most people make grad-school friends through their lab and
department, primarily on account of proximity. Your department
probably has some kind of grad-student social committee that
plans events and get-togethers, and they are a great opportunity
to introduce yourself, spark some friendships, and get to know
more about the department. Intra- and interdepartmental sport-
ing events are another popular avenue for socializing.

You also shouldn't discount the value of getting to know some
of the locals. After a few years in grad school, I developed closely
knit friendships with many locals in town (thanks to a serendipitous trip to the piano store, of all things). These friends revealed
all of the exciting goings-on that the university students rarely
learned about. There was hiking, civic theater, farmers' markets,
Christmas parades down Main Street, public fairs, tours of the old
mansions, corn mazes, hipster bars without a single undergrad.
Enhancing my social circle away from the university made it possible to participate in an established community, rather than in
only the makeshift circles assembled by mutually suffering grad
students. Incidentally, it was also locals who introduced me to my
wife, who herself was also a grad student, but in a discipline so
far removed from mine that we never would have crossed paths
on campus.

Bottom line: the only person who can stand in the way of your
social life is you. The closest friends I have ever had are those I

made in grad school, and I know many people who would say the same. But I also know people who let grad school get the better of them, who let the pressures of classes, research, and an over-bearing advisor eat into their souls until every ounce of happiness was extinguished. And for all that suffering, many of these people also didn't finish grad school.

When I was an undergrad, I occasionally asked my professors about grad school, and their first reaction to my question always involved their eyes widening in terror. You may have seen this deer-in-the-headlights look yourself, and I fear that it turns many people off from grad school before they have a chance to learn anything substantive about it. Far too many people look back on grad school as a time of suffering, when there is no money, no time, no sleep, no respect. But I firmly believe that you do not have to be miserable in grad school. Your happiness, however, is up to you. Life, work, and the real world are going to come at you ten times worse than anything a university throws at you, so you better figure out how to be happy with your "half-time" life as a grad student if you want any hope of enjoying your *real* life after it.

About the Author

Joseph Gangestad is the author of several scholarly journal articles in the fields of aerospace engineering and astrodynamics and has authored the articles on "Celestial Mechanics" and "Orbital Motion" for the *McGraw-Hill Encyclopedia of Science and Technology*. A native of Boston, Massachusetts, he received his bachelor's degree in Astrophysics from Williams College, a liberal arts college in western Massachusetts, and later a master's degree and Ph.D. in Aeronautical & Astronautical Engineering from Purdue University in West Lafayette, Indiana. Dr. Gangestad currently works in the aerospace industry in southern California.

Made in the USA
Lexington, KY
30 April 2015